# MAN LAW

**Chris Walker**

# Contents

# PREFACE

Welcome to *Man Law: Unveiling the Principles of Masculinity.* In today's world, being a man is no easy feat. As we navigate the complexities of modern society, it becomes essential to revisit the fundamental concepts from our past that help define manhood. This book delves into the realm of man laws, specifically tailored for those aspiring to embody the qualities of an alpha male, or what many would consider a real man.

It is important to note that some of the topics discussed in this book may push the boundaries of comfort and challenge conventional thinking. However, these discussions should be approached with an open mind, as they are intended to provoke thought and encourage introspection. This book is a personal reflection of my journey, written to inspire other men to better understand the unique challenges we face.

In an era where the so-called alpha woman asserts her place in the world, it becomes vital for men to recognize the importance of adhering to these man laws. In the past, men were expected to marry, build families, and fulfill their roles as providers. Even then, they were expected to abide by certain principles that demonstrated their masculinity, self-control, and ability to lead.

Sadly, over time, some of these core concepts appear to have been lost or overshadowed. The changing dynamics of our society, coupled with the absence of fathers in many households, have contributed to a generation of men grappling with their identities and emotions. The responsibility of teaching young men how to be men often falls on single mothers who, despite their best efforts, cannot fully impart certain skills, perspectives, and experiences that a father traditionally provides.

In *Man Law*, we explore the significance of these lost concepts and examine the principles that define true masculinity. It is my intention to guide men on a journey of self-discovery and provide them with the tools necessary to navigate the challenges of modern masculinity. Within these pages, you will find 50 fundamental laws that encapsulate the essence of manhood.

Through these laws, we will explore the principles that define us as men. From embracing resilience to embodying self-sufficiency, each law reveals an essential aspect of manhood. While many other principles contribute to our understanding of masculinity, these first 50 serve as the foundation upon which we can build a fulfilling and purposeful life.

I invite you to embark on this transformative journey with me. As you read through the pages of *Man Law*, may you gain new insights, challenge your beliefs, and ultimately discover a renewed sense of purpose as a man. Let us reclaim the principles that define us and embrace the responsibilities and privileges that come with being a man.

# CHAPTER 1
## Think With Logic, Not Emotions

In today's world, it is crucial for men to learn to think with logic rather than being driven solely by their emotions. Let me illustrate this with an incident that occurred during the Oscars. Chris Rock made a joke about Jada Pinkett Smith, and her husband, Will Smith, became furious and attempted to slap Chris Rock on stage. However, this act of anger not only brought Chris Rock more attention and financial gain, but also cast Will Smith in a negative light.

Will Smith, whether you like it or not, is looked up to by many as a role model of masculinity. Yet his attempt to physically harm someone demonstrated a lack of self-control and revealed a weakness within him. While it may appear manly to resort to violence, it is, in fact, a cowardly act. Instead of giving in to his emotions, Will Smith should have relied on logic. Logic would have reminded him that anger rarely leads to a positive outcome. Rather, that energy could have been channeled into something more productive, such as focusing on his work, showing love to his family, or pursuing a meaningful mission.

Interestingly, even his wife, Jada Pinkett Smith, criticized his actions afterward. She stated that he was wrong to have slapped Chris Rock and that she was capable of handling the situation herself. Will Smith's behavior exemplifies the emasculated man, someone who tries so hard to please his wife that he ultimately relinquishes his own power and authority.

By embracing logic, we can simplify and address issues more effectively. Acting on emotion often leads to more problems and a lack of inner peace. It can be compared to belittling or disrespecting a woman, something real men do not do. A real man assesses the situation and decides whether to engage in a conversation or simply walk away. How many times have we been lured into fights by women, not realizing that they operate primarily on emotion? Engaging in fights or arguments benefits no one involved, so why bother?

Jesus expressed this idea clearly when he said, "Turn the other cheek." This teaching is not about fear or cowardice. It reflects an understanding that what someone feels in one moment may not be the same the next day. It takes intuition to recognize that negativity directed toward you often reflects the other person's pain.

Women may try to provoke anger, especially during breakups. At times they may deliberately push your buttons, knowing that your reactions can later be used against you in divorce proceedings. In situations like these, the best course of action is to let it go. Recognize that the woman may be hurting, and the most powerful response is often to ignore the provocation. When you ignore someone, you place yourself in a different space, detached from their negativity. While they remain angry, you are free to live your life and pursue happiness. No one can truly affect you unless you allow them to affect your psyche.

Emotions are fickle and can change from one moment to the next. This is why thinking logically is essential. Regardless of how someone feels, the truth remains constant. Some people struggle to handle the truth, but as men, we must strive to understand and embrace it.

In the chapters that follow, we will explore the principles of manhood in greater depth, examining how logic, self-control, and understanding can shape our lives and relationships. By embracing these principles, we can navigate the complexities of modern masculinity with confidence and purpose.

# CHAPTER 2
## Understanding The Complexities Of Relationships

In this chapter, we will explore the complexities of relationships and the importance of understanding the dynamics between men and women. These topics require an open mind and a willingness to question certain societal assumptions.

The notion that women are the devil is a misguided belief rooted in a narrow interpretation of biblical stories. It is important to remember that the Bible contains many allegorical narratives that convey deeper lessons about the human experience. The story of Adam and Eve, for example, can be understood as a metaphor for human choice, temptation, and responsibility rather than a literal justification for demonizing women.

Relationships can be challenging, and both men and women are capable of negative behavior. However, portraying all women as untrustworthy or self-centered is unfair and reinforces harmful stereotypes. People are complex individuals who should be evaluated by their actions and character, not by assumptions tied to gender.

Healthy relationships are built on trust, respect, and open communication. Both men and women possess the ability to love deeply and remain loyal to their partners. Generalizing from negative experiences or assumptions only creates division and misunderstanding. A more constructive approach is to seek mutual understanding and practice empathy.

The belief that men are naturally more loyal than women is also a misconception. Loyalty is not determined by gender but by personal values and integrity. Both men and women are capable of loyalty or betrayal. The key to strong relationships lies in cultivating trust through honesty, accountability, and consistent communication rather than relying on broad generalizations.

Marriage, contrary to the belief presented, is not simply a materialistic contract that limits freedom. It is a commitment between two individuals who choose to build a life together. While marriage may not be the right path for everyone, it can provide a strong foundation for love, support, and personal growth.

It is crucial to approach relationships with self-love and self-respect. A man should not lose himself within a relationship but should instead strive to maintain a healthy balance between individuality and partnership. Both partners should support and uplift one another rather than seek validation or attempt to gain power over each other.

It is also important to challenge societal expectations and stereotypes. Men should not feel confined to rigid roles such as being solely the provider or the alpha male. Likewise, women should not be limited to playing the victim or expecting someone else to rescue them. Each individual should be encouraged to pursue personal passions, dreams, and growth.

In conclusion, relationships are complex and should be approached with understanding and empathy. Both men and women are capable of love, loyalty, and meaningful personal growth. By challenging stereotypes and embracing individuality, we can build healthy and fulfilling relationships grounded in mutual respect and support.

# CHAPTER 3
## The Importance Of Living Below Your Means

In this chapter, we will explore the significance of living below your means and the impact it can have on your overall well-being and success. It is important to understand that true success is not measured by material possessions but by personal growth and fulfillment.

Growing up in a prominent family, I was accustomed to having everything I desired. However, as I grew older, I realized that material possessions do not define success. It is easy to be enticed by the allure of expensive cars, luxurious houses, and extravagant lifestyles, but these things do not guarantee happiness or fulfillment.

Living below your means involves making conscious decisions about how you spend your money. It means prioritizing investments in yourself, such as education, personal development, and experiences that enrich your life. It is not about depriving yourself, but about making wise choices that align with your long-term goals and values.

Regardless of how much money you have, whether it is one million dollars or only a few dollars, it is important to remember that wealth is relative. What truly matters is how you use your resources to build a meaningful and purposeful life. Success should not be measured by material possessions but by the growth you achieve and the impact you have on yourself and others.

It is important to detach yourself from the belief that your worth is determined by what others think of you or by the things you own. True success comes from within and is defined by your character, integrity, and the positive contributions you make to the world.

In conclusion, living below your means is a mindset that allows you to prioritize what truly matters in life. It involves investing in yourself, pursuing personal growth, and finding fulfillment beyond material possessions. By embracing this philosophy, you can create a life that is rich in experiences, meaningful relationships, and personal achievements.

# CHAPTER 4

## You Will Never Find The Right Person; You Must Become The Right Person

In our quest for love, we often find ourselves searching for that perfect person who will complete us. We hear about soulmates and twin flames, but I challenge these ideas. The truth is that there's no such thing as a soulmate or a twin flame. We'll never find someone who perfectly matches us because the key to finding the right person lies within ourselves.

Before entering relationships, especially for men seeking women, it's crucial to embark on a journey of self-discovery and self-improvement. Take a step back from dating and dedicate at least a year to understanding who you are at your core. Explore your values, your likes, and your dislikes. Focus on strengthening yourself physically, mentally, and emotionally.

To attract the partner you desire, you must first become the person you aspire to be. Just as a mirror reflects our image, life reflects our inner state. Like attracts like, and you'll inevitably attract what you embody. If you seek a faithful and caring woman, you must first learn to care for and value yourself. The energy you cultivate internally will manifest externally and shape the relationships you attract.

On the other hand, if you prefer casual relationships and enjoy exploring different connections, there's no shame in that. Embrace your preferences and be honest with yourself. However, understand that the quality of the women you attract will often reflect your own values and behavior. Don't be surprised if you encounter unfaithfulness or dissatisfaction in your relationships when you haven't first been faithful to yourself.

It's essential to acknowledge that, as individuals, we evolve and grow throughout life. Sometimes the person we marry or commit to may not grow in the same direction we do. To reduce the chances of this happening, seek partners who share your goals, values, and standards. Make sure your paths align, not only at the beginning but throughout the journey. Being selective becomes crucial when choosing the right woman to walk that path with you.

Remember, not everything that glitters is gold, and not every woman who stands out is comfortable within herself. Each person carries different perspectives, values, and preferences. We are all unique individuals, and there is no perfect match waiting somewhere in the world. Instead, we should focus on becoming the best versions of ourselves.

Men often make the mistake of seeking a woman before truly finding themselves. They rush into relationships before reaching the right place in life. Instead of focusing on personal growth and progress, they become entangled in the struggles that can come with a relationship. It's important to prioritize personal development and build stability before adding someone else to the equation.

For men searching for the right woman, allow connections to develop naturally. Don't chase women. Instead, pursue your own success, financial stability, and personal freedom. When your life is in order, women will naturally gravitate toward you. Many are drawn to stability and security, qualities that a man demonstrates when he knows what he wants and can provide for himself and potentially for a family.

Remember, you don't attract what you want. You attract what you are. Rather than searching endlessly for the perfect person, focus on becoming the best version of yourself. As you continue on this journey of self-discovery and personal growth, the right woman will eventually find her way into your life. Keep growing, keep improving, and remain open to the love that may come your way.

# CHAPTER 5
## Choose Your Hard

---

Life is undoubtedly challenging. Throughout our journey, we encounter numerous obstacles such as family issues, financial struggles, work pressures, and even the inevitability of death. As men, it's crucial to understand the concept of choosing our hard. By prioritizing and confronting difficult tasks head-on, we can pave the way for a smoother and more rewarding life in the future.

Doing hard things takes courage. It's human nature to seek the path of least resistance and choose the easy way out. However, this approach rarely leads to an easier life. It's easy to fall into an unhealthy lifestyle and become overweight, but it's hard to commit to regular exercise. It's easy to spend money carelessly and end up broke, but it's hard to save and build financial stability. It's easy to neglect our relationships, but it's hard to face the consequences of loneliness. The key is to choose our hard consciously.

Reflecting on my own journey, I must admit that I often chose the easy route. I dreamed of making it to the NFL, but I wasn't willing to put in the necessary work. I aspired to attend a prestigious Division I college, but I hesitated to sacrifice my social life for academic success. As I matured, however, I realized that as men, we can't afford to complain or dwell on what could have been. We must take responsibility for our actions and prioritize what truly matters.

More often than not, success comes to those who choose the harder path. Instead of procrastinating or giving in to temporary pleasures, successful men demonstrate discipline and determination. They understand that life is full of challenges, and it's through perseverance that growth and achievement take place. Many even become grateful for the hardships they've endured, because those experiences shape them into the men they eventually become.

On the other hand, an average man tends to blame external factors for his circumstances. He may envy those who have achieved great success and wonder why he hasn't been similarly blessed. However, it's important to recognize that God favors those who take action and put in the effort. Faith and prayer are powerful, but they must be accompanied by hard work. God places obstacles in our path to make us stronger and wiser, and it's through learning from our mistakes that we grow and develop.

Mistakes are invaluable because they teach us some of life's most important lessons. If we were to win all the time, we would never truly understand the growth that comes from setbacks. It may take a thousand losses to achieve a single victory, but that victory becomes far more meaningful because of the lessons learned along the way.

As men, we attract what we are. If we aren't willing to make sacrifices for our own improvement, we can't expect greatness to come our way. Many men become infatuated with the superficial aspects of life such as material possessions, women, or substances. However, those who possess self-control and discipline are the ones who truly shape their circumstances and achieve lasting success. Just as resistance builds muscle in the gym, embracing the hard things in life builds character and strength.

Consider the example of money management. If you were to give a man a million dollars, he might squander it within six months. In contrast, a man who has already achieved financial success would likely use that same million dollars to multiply his wealth. This difference exists because he has learned the importance of discipline and consistency through his own journey.

He understands that money is a tool, not merely a possession, and he has developed the knowledge to use it wisely.

Choosing your hard is a fundamental principle in life. If you choose the easy path, life will eventually become more difficult. I am now 37 years old and have been diagnosed with sciatica, a condition that limits my physical activity. The doctor advised me not to exercise, run, or engage in strenuous activities. However, I chose not to accept that limitation. Every day, I fight against my physical constraints in order to live as normally as possible.

I have friends my age who struggle with health issues and constant stress because they choose to work endlessly and cope by drowning their sorrows in alcohol. As men, it's our responsibility to take care of ourselves because our bodies are the vehicles that carry us through life. To achieve good health, we must be willing to put in the effort and make the necessary sacrifices.

In today's world, social media has become a platform for comparison and validation. Many people project an image of a luxurious and glamorous life that often contradicts their actual reality. As men, we don't have time for such façades. If we are truly living fulfilling lives, we are too busy being present in the moment to seek external validation. Our actions and accomplishments should speak for themselves. True fulfillment comes from within, through personal growth and self-improvement.

Life's outcomes are not determined solely by external factors such as wealth or status. Instead, they are shaped by our internal momentum. Material success is often a reflection of the discipline, character, and mindset that develop within us over time.

# CHAPTER 6

## Life Is Like Driving a Car

Life is like driving a car, a metaphorical journey that reflects the experiences and challenges we encounter as we navigate the twists and turns of existence. Just as a driver begins a road trip with a destination in mind, individuals embark on their own unique journeys toward personal fulfillment and self-discovery.

Imagine yourself behind the wheel of a car, ready to begin an adventure. To reach your destination, you need a few essentials. First, you need fuel. In life, this fuel comes in the form of goals that provide the motivation and drive to move forward. These goals sustain you throughout the journey and give you the energy and determination to overcome obstacles and keep progressing.

Just as a driver relies on a GPS to navigate unfamiliar roads, in life you need a clear sense of direction and purpose. This internal GPS guides your decisions and actions, helping you make choices that align with your values and aspirations. It serves as a compass that provides clarity and leads you along the path toward personal growth and fulfillment.

As you continue your journey, you must keep your focus on the road ahead. Looking back for too long can be dangerous because it may cause you to lose sight of what lies in front of you. Dwelling on the past can lead to crashes and detours that prevent progress and limit new opportunities. However, it's still important to glance at the rearview mirror from time to time. The purpose is not to dwell on past mistakes, but to learn from them and avoid repeating them. Reflection allows us to gain wisdom and make better decisions as we continue navigating the road ahead.

Staying in your lane is crucial, both in driving and in life. When you stay in your lane, you remain focused on your own path and avoid unnecessary collisions or conflicts with others. It's essential to focus on your own journey without comparing yourself to the progress or achievements of others. Each person has their own unique timeline and destination, and it's important to respect and support one another's individual paths.

Along the way, you may encounter various pit stops and rest areas. These pit stops represent moments in life when you need to pause, reflect, and address any challenges or obstacles that arise. Just as a car requires regular maintenance, you also need time to repair and nurture yourself. These pit stops allow you to recharge, gain perspective, and make any necessary adjustments to ensure a smooth and safe journey.

Choosing the right passengers to accompany you on your journey is crucial. Surrounding yourself with supportive and like-minded individuals can make the journey more enjoyable and fulfilling. They can serve as co-navigators, guiding you toward the best routes and offering encouragement when the road gets rough. On the other hand, the wrong passengers can become distractions that lead you off course and hinder your progress. It's important to choose companions who share your values and aspirations, individuals who will uplift and inspire you on your path.

Just as cars come in different shapes and sizes, individuals also have unique circumstances and backgrounds. Regardless of the vehicle you drive, as long as it is well maintained and driven with determination, it can reach its destination. Similarly, in life, everyone has the potential to achieve their goals and aspirations. It's not our external circumstances that define us, but our mindset, resilience, and commitment to the journey.

Throughout your personal road trip, you may encounter breakdowns and detours. These moments test your resilience and provide opportunities for growth and learning. They help you develop problem-solving skills, adaptability, and perseverance. Embracing these challenges and using them as stepping stones can lead to personal transformation and a deeper understanding of yourself.

Unlike driving a car, life doesn't have a definitive destination. It is an ongoing journey of self-discovery, growth, and continuous exploration. The process itself holds immense value and meaning. It is during the journey that we learn, evolve, and uncover our true potential. Each experience, whether joyful or challenging, contributes to the richness and depth of our lives.

So as you navigate the roads of life, remember to keep your tank full of goals and aspirations, trust your internal GPS, focus on the road ahead, stay in your lane, make necessary pit stops to refuel and repair, choose your companions wisely, and embrace the unexpected detours and challenges that come your way. Enjoy the journey, because it is along the journey that you will find purpose, growth, and the beauty of the unknown. Remember that shortcuts often lead nowhere.

# CHAPTER 7
## The Shortcuts That Lead Nowhere

A h, the good old days of childhood mischief and clever schemes. Remember when you would clean your room in a hurry by shoving everything into the closet just to impress your parents? And of course, when they opened that closet door, chaos followed as all your hidden treasures spilled out, leaving you to clean up the mess all over again. It was a classic example of taking a shortcut that led nowhere.

But that wasn't the only time shortcuts came back to haunt us. Who could forget the thrill of cheating on a test as a child and miraculously earning a perfect score? It felt as if we had outsmarted the system. However, when the final exam arrived, where cheating was strictly forbidden, we often found ourselves on our own, unable to rely on those same shortcuts. In hindsight, those moments perfectly capture the essence of this chapter. Shortcuts may get you to a result faster, but they rob you of the valuable experience and knowledge gained along the way.

I've had my fair share of encounters with shortcuts, especially in my line of work. As a writer, I've been approached by students who wanted me to write their college papers for them. I always felt it was important to remind them that while I could help them earn a good grade, they would miss out on the essential knowledge and skills required for their field of study. It's like taking a shortcut through a maze. You may reach the end quickly, but you won't develop the ability to navigate similar challenges in the future.

Shortcuts can be tempting. They promise to save time and help us accomplish more. However, they often come at a high cost.

If you choose to take a shortcut, you should be prepared to face the consequences. My father once taught me that if you don't do something right the first time, you'll end up having to do it all over again. Shortcuts leave room for mistakes and often become more time-consuming than doing things the right way from the beginning.

Moreover, shortcuts can have damaging effects on our relationships and finances. If we rely on dishonest means, such as stealing or manipulating others, it will eventually catch up with us. Trust will be broken and bridges will be burned. The relationships and opportunities we might have gained through honest hard work will disappear. Shortcuts rob us of the sense of achievement and confidence that come from overcoming obstacles and completing tasks with diligence.

Consider the cautionary tale of a young man who managed to cheat his way through high school. He nearly achieved a perfect GPA and gained admission to several prestigious colleges. However, once he arrived at college, he found himself unable to keep up with the workload and the demands of projects that required more than memorizing answers for tests. The shortcut strategy that worked in high school failed completely in the more demanding college environment. Eventually, he dropped out and moved back in with his parents. His story serves as a stark reminder of the consequences of relying on shortcuts.

Taking shortcuts is similar to lying. It may seem easier in the moment, but it often leads to greater stress and complications later on. Cutting corners might appear to save time or effort, but it ultimately undermines long-term success. If we truly want to achieve greatness in life, we must be willing to embrace every step of the process from start to finish. It's perfectly acceptable to seek help from others, as long as that help doesn't involve cheating or bypassing essential steps.

Sometimes, shortcuts can even harm others. Imagine starting a business and finding an investor who believes in your vision.

They provide the necessary funds to help your venture get off the ground. However, instead of honoring your commitment to repay them, you decide to take a shortcut and avoid paying them back. This decision can lead not only to legal consequences but also to broken trust and damaged relationships. Regardless of whether your business succeeds or fails, you should always fulfill your obligations and repay those who supported you. Taking shortcuts with other people's money is a sure way to damage relationships and close doors that you may need in the future.

In the end, the best approach is to remain honest with ourselves and with others. When we begin any endeavor, we should fully understand the process and commit to completing each step without relying on shortcuts. Yes, shortcuts may promise a faster route, but they leave us empty-handed when it comes to the knowledge, growth, and sense of accomplishment that come from dedication and hard work. So, dear reader, remember the lesson of this chapter. Shortcuts may seem tempting, but they lead nowhere. Embrace the journey and appreciate the rewards that come from doing things the right way from start to finish.

# CHAPTER 8

## Life Is Math: Either We Are Adding, Subtracting, Multiplying, Or Dividing (The Law Of Accumulation)

Life is essentially like a math equation, where you're constantly adding, subtracting, multiplying, or dividing your experiences and relationships. If you want a solid perspective on how to navigate the complexities of human interaction and existence, studying math can offer surprisingly profound insights. Math represents a form of ultimate truth. It doesn't lie, and $1 + 1$ will always equal 2. There are no exceptions. Now consider how this mathematical precision connects to the messiness of life. Every day, you're either multiplying your joys and strengths or subtracting from your happiness and potential. Understanding this concept can reveal valuable lessons about building relationships and succeeding in life.

Take a toxic friendship, for example. If you find yourself in a relationship that constantly drains you, it's likely subtracting from your overall well-being or even dividing you from your true purpose. In contrast, a good friend adds value to your life and multiplies your happiness, enriching your journey. Think about the act of adding. It reflects the law of accumulation. Engaging in good habits like exercising, excelling at your job, or being a supportive parent allows positive actions to accumulate over time, leading to personal growth and fulfillment.

On the other hand, if you're waking up at noon, indulging in junk food, and making poor life choices, the law of accumulation still applies, just in the opposite direction. You're subtracting from your happiness and health, and eventually that lifestyle will catch up with you. Multiplication is where things become even more powerful. It reflects the idea of synergy. When two people work together, their combined efforts can produce results far greater than either could achieve alone. Think of it like a chain reaction. 1 person influences 3 others, and before long, the positive impact begins to multiply exponentially.

Division also plays a critical role. You might encounter individuals in your life who divide you from your purpose, breaking down relationships or undermining your happiness. In a marriage, if your partner is not supportive, they can divide your focus and ambitions, leading to emotional chaos. But just as you can add positive influences to your life, you can also subtract negative ones. Sometimes, simply standing still and allowing life to unfold can be the most powerful action.

The same principle applies to multiplication. A series of positive habits can compound into a life of joy and success, while a series of bad habits can lead to a downward spiral of misery. Division works in a similar way. Removing toxic influences from your life can create space for growth and new opportunities. In many ways, life is a process of accumulation, and it often comes down to simple math.

To truly grasp these concepts, take a moment to reflect on your life. Write down the people, places, and activities that fill your days, and categorize them as adding, multiplying, subtracting, or dividing. There's no absolute right answer, only your truth. When you understand the law of accumulation and observe how these factors affect your life, you can begin to rebuild it with intention and purpose. Remember, the only things you can truly control in this vast universe are your mind and your actions. You cannot dictate how others behave or how they may try to influence you. So harness this remarkable mathematical principle and apply

it to your life, because it holds the potential for remarkable
transformation.

# CHAPTER 9
## The Importance Of Family

Family is a multifaceted and essential part of our lives, intricately woven into the fabric of our existence. It serves as both a sanctuary and a battleground, offering unwavering support while also challenging us in ways that can sometimes feel overwhelming. The bonds we share with family are often unbreakable, providing a steady home base from which we navigate the complexities of life. These individuals, who know us better than anyone else, act as mirrors that reflect both our strengths and our weaknesses. Their insights can be harsh, but they are often rooted in deep love and a genuine desire to see us succeed. While we may clash with them at times and experience moments of frustration, it's important to recognize that this love is a cornerstone of our personal development.

Siblings, in particular, hold a unique place in our lives. No matter how successful we become or where life takes us, they often continue to see us through the lens of our shared childhood experiences. They remember the innocent mischief, the sibling rivalries, and the countless memories that bind us together. This shared history creates a sense of belonging that is difficult to replicate outside of family. Even when I found myself cast as the "black sheep," my family stood by me, offering both support and unfiltered honesty rather than empty compliments. Their willingness to confront my shortcomings, from my struggles with addiction to my academic pursuits, showed a commitment to my well-being that I've come to appreciate deeply. They didn't hesitate to tell me when I was off course. Instead, they helped me face difficult truths about myself, making sure I had the perspective and support needed to make meaningful changes.

However, it's important to acknowledge that not all family interactions are positive or nurturing. At times, family members may display toxic behaviors that hinder personal growth and well-being. Recognizing when to step back from these unhealthy dynamics is essential, even while understanding that family ties are often difficult to sever completely. Forgiveness becomes an important skill in these situations. Understanding that no one can replace the unique connection we share with our family members can help us navigate these emotions more effectively. It's important to value those relationships, even when they are filled with tension, because they often shape the foundation of our personal stories.

In moments of despair, family can become our greatest source of motivation. They remind us of our worth and potential, helping us rise from our lowest points. The power of their encouragement can be profound. When you know your family believes in you, it can inspire you to keep pushing through adversity. Each of us faces challenges that may seem overwhelming, but the knowledge that our family stands behind us can make a significant difference. They often carry wisdom gained from their own life experiences and can offer valuable lessons about love, resilience, and respect.

Life is complicated, and it can feel especially isolating when we face hardships without a support system. Those fortunate enough to have family know they're not alone. They have a safety net, a group of people who will catch them when they stumble. This safety net is not merely a passive presence. It's an active force in our lives that encourages us to learn, grow, and ultimately succeed. Embracing family means recognizing that, despite our differences and occasional conflicts, these relationships are irreplaceable. They shape our identity and provide the foundation upon which we build our lives.

When I reflect on my life, I often think about the lessons I've learned from my family, both good and bad. They've taught me the importance of humility, the value of hard work, and the necessity of accountability. If there's one thing I could change, it would be listening to my parents' advice more closely when I was younger. At the time, I often believed I knew better and thought I could forge my own path without their guidance. As I've grown older, however, I've realized that their wisdom is a treasure trove of insight that could have saved me from many of my struggles.

# CHAPTER 10
## The Psychology Of Women

Throughout my life, I've made it a personal quest to understand women. Spoiler alert: it's like trying to solve a Rubik's Cube blindfolded while riding a unicycle. Women are beautifully complex and often appear as walking contradictions, and that isn't necessarily a bad thing. So buckle up, gentlemen. This ride is going to take us through the labyrinthine psychology of women.

**The Heart vs. Logic Dichotomy**

First, let's get one thing straight. Men and women often operate on different wavelengths. Men tend to rely more on logic, while women frequently navigate life through their feelings. This difference can create misunderstandings that would make even the most experienced diplomat cringe. Women may say one thing, but their decisions often come from a deeply emotional place. For example, a woman might strongly criticize cheating while at the same time finding herself involved as someone's "side piece." It's a puzzling contradiction, but it also reflects the complexity of human behavior.

Some women remain in verbally or physically abusive relationships, sometimes sacrificing their emotional well-being in exchange for financial security or stability. Loyalty can be a complicated concept in these situations. Many women remain loyal to how they feel in the moment rather than to any particular individual. This isn't necessarily an insult or criticism; it's simply part of how emotions can influence decisions. At times, women may even struggle to get along with one another. It's not uncommon to hear friends gossip about each other. Yet those same women may still base their decisions on the opinions of other women, creating a fascinating web of contradictions.

## Lessons from Marriage and Divorce

I used to fall head over heels for women, but my marriage and subsequent divorce turned out to be my greatest teachers. It became crystal clear to me what many women desire: security and affirmation. This is why phrases like "Happy wife, happy life" exist. In reality, many men find themselves in situations where they feel they must agree with their wives simply to avoid conflict.

This is exactly why I'm hesitant to get married again. I might wait until I'm in my fifties or sixties because, by then, I'll likely be more interested in companionship than in the complexities of romantic entanglements.

## The Nature of Male-Female Relationships

Men often crave companionship but can sometimes find women frustrating. If it weren't for physical attraction, many guys might not even bother. Still, I can't dismiss the fact that women can make excellent friends, at least until you piss them off.

I'm not here to repeat the same old rhetoric you hear on male-dominated podcasts. I'm simply keeping it real. I genuinely love women for their unpredictability because it keeps me on my toes. These days I date multiple women, and it's a deliberate choice. I've learned that a woman can leave at a moment's notice.

## The Cat-and-Mouse Game

Here's a universal truth: to keep a woman, she must care more about you than you care about her. It sounds harsh, but it's true. If you have a roster of women, be prepared for the inevitable three-month mark when one of them will demand a relationship. If you don't comply, she might leave.

The ones who truly care will leave and return multiple times, reflecting the feline nature of love: if you chase a cat, it will always elude you.

Letting women come to you is key. Confidence is attractive, but ultimately they choose you; you don't choose them. Signs a woman is interested include lingering gazes and positioning herself to engage you in conversation. It's a delicate dance of attraction, often muddled by the duality of love and hate. A woman can simultaneously love and hate you, which is as chaotic as it sounds.

**Societal Dynamics and Women's Influence**

In today's world, men are waking up to these dynamics. Many are focusing on self-improvement and discipline, often influenced by podcasts and motivational speakers. Women, on the other hand, might find themselves glued to reality TV, indulging in drama that feeds the chaos in their lives.

While the current wave of female rappers dominates pop culture, it's important to recognize the duality they exhibit. Yes, women can be a source of chaos, but they can also provide incredible peace and insight. A good woman can help you grow and nurture your ambitions without demanding anything in return.

**The Quest for the Right Woman**

However, the reality is that not all women fit this mold. Roughly 90% can be self-centered, focused on their immediate desires. And while I'm not a woman-basher, it's crucial for men to discern what they want in a partner.

If you aspire to have a family and a lasting marriage, finding the right woman is essential. Otherwise, you risk ending up in a "paternity soup" of obligations and divorce courts that tend to favor women.

Avoid unnecessary conflict. Women thrive on drama. When you're in a disagreement, sometimes the best move is to walk away and return when emotions have cooled. This allows for a more rational conversation later.

## Strength Amidst Vulnerability

Never, under any circumstances, resort to physical violence. Hitting a woman is not only cowardly, but it is also a surefire way to lose respect. Men are generally stronger physically, and that is a reality. Emotional confrontations can be just as damaging. Constant arguing lowers you to a level that many women do not respect. Women are often attracted to men who are strong, confident, and capable.

You have probably seen it yourself. The men who seem to attract women effortlessly usually carry themselves with confidence and a clear sense of purpose. They understand an important principle: love yourself first. When you project self-assurance, women naturally gravitate toward that energy.

## Final Thoughts

At the end of the day, the universe doesn't distinguish between good and bad intentions in the way we might think. It often responds to effort, focus, and consistency. If you are the type of "nice guy" who allows women to walk all over you, it should not be surprising if you eventually find yourself feeling unappreciated or alone.

Women tend to respect men who stand firm in their boundaries. When you set limits and communicate them clearly, many women will respect those boundaries. You do not need to overwhelm them with gifts or compliments to earn their appreciation. In many cases, women value a man who can provide protection, emotional stability, and a strong sense of self.

So, gentlemen, the choice is yours. Take the time to understand the psychology of women, embrace the complexities, and focus on becoming the best version of yourself. When you do that, you place yourself in a position to attract the kind of woman who aligns with the life you want to build.

## The Science of Women and Practical Solutions

Delving deeper into the psychology of women reveals layers of complexity and nuance that can enrich our understanding of relationships. Below are several key themes worth exploring.

## Emotional Landscape

## 1.  Feelings as Law

Women often use their emotions as guiding principles when making decisions. Unlike men, who may rely more heavily on logic, women frequently evaluate situations through the lens of how they feel. This emotional awareness can sometimes lead to decisions that appear contradictory to outsiders. Understanding this dynamic can help men navigate conversations and conflicts more effectively.

## 2.  Communication Styles

Women often communicate their feelings indirectly. They may offer hints or expect their partners to read between the lines. This can be frustrating for men who tend to prefer direct communication. Recognizing this difference can encourage clearer dialogue and reduce misunderstandings.

## Relationship Dynamics

## 1. The Role of Security

Many women look for emotional and financial security in relationships. This desire has roots in evolutionary psychology, where stability has historically been associated with survival. Men who can provide a sense of safety, both emotionally and physically, are often perceived as more attractive partners.

## 2. Duality of Love and Hate

Emotional fluctuations can create situations where love and frustration coexist. This dynamic can be confusing, but it also reflects the depth of emotional investment women may have in their relationships. It is not unusual for a woman to express irritation or anger while still caring deeply about the person involved.

## Social Influences

## 1. Cultural Expectations

Societal expectations often place pressure on women to conform to certain ideals, whether related to appearance, behavior, or career paths. These pressures can create internal conflicts that lead women to act in ways that may seem inconsistent with their true desires.

## 2. Media Representation

The way women are portrayed in media, including reality television and popular music, can shape perceptions and expectations. These portrayals often highlight drama and conflict, which can influence how women interpret relationships, identity, and self-worth.

## Personal Growth and Independence

## 1. Empowerment through Self-Discovery

Many women are actively engaged in a process of self-discovery and empowerment. This journey often involves redefining traditional roles and expectations. Women who develop a strong sense of independence can become supportive partners because they understand the importance of personal growth.

## 2. Choosing the Right Partner

Women often seek partners who respect their autonomy and support their ambitions. A partner who encourages personal development and shares similar values is more likely to contribute to a healthy and lasting relationship.

## Navigating Relationships

## 1. Importance of Boundaries

Establishing and respecting boundaries is essential in any relationship. Women often appreciate men who can assert themselves and set clear limits. This creates a foundation built on mutual respect and understanding.

## 2. The Attraction of Confidence

Confidence is a powerful and attractive quality. Women are often drawn to men who are self-assured and comfortable with who they are. This doesn't mean being arrogant. Instead, it means having a strong sense of self-worth and being secure in your identity.

## Final Thoughts

Understanding the psychology of women is not about placing them in a box or labeling them as one thing or another. Rather, it involves recognizing the complex mix of emotions, societal influences, and personal experiences that shape their behaviors and desires.

As men navigate their relationships, embracing empathy and maintaining an open mind can lead to deeper connections. By encouraging honest communication and mutual understanding, both people in the relationship can build a more balanced and fulfilling partnership where each person feels respected and heard.

# CHAPTER 11

## God Will Give You Big Lessons For Small Mistakes

You know how people say not to sweat the small things? I see it a little differently. To me, if you can't handle the small tasks, you'll never be able to handle the big ones. Small mistakes often lead to bigger ones down the road.

Right now, I'm teaching my daughter about being financially responsible. Like many sixth-graders, she used to spend her money on things like Roblox and little knickknacks. The truth is, those things don't last, and the money disappears quickly. So I decided to step in and open a bank account for her. Her mom and I both keep an eye on it, making sure she saves most of what she earns and only spends a small portion.

I want her to understand early in life that she can't rely on other people for her financial security. She needs to learn how to take care of herself. If she continues developing the right habits now, she won't grow up depending on someone else to provide for her.

The small money habits she's learning today will shape her financial future. Living below your means is one of the most important lessons a person can learn. They don't teach that in most schools, but life certainly does.

**Small Money Habits, Big Financial Impact**

Let me tell you something: the small things we do every day matter. Making your bed, brushing your teeth, taking a shower, and keeping yourself presentable all seem simple. Missing a day or two might not feel like a big deal, but if it turns into a habit, it can lead to an unhealthy lifestyle, poor hygiene, and bigger problems over time. Those little things add up.

In my own life, I've made small mistakes that turned into serious issues. One example was drinking and driving. I only wanted to visit a friend who lived down the street, but that one decision ended up costing me thousands of dollars in legal fees.

When I was younger, I also didn't pay enough attention to what I ate. As an athlete, if I had taken my nutrition and training more seriously, I might have had a real chance at making it to the NFL. Now, at 37 years old, I see friends my age dealing with heart problems, high blood pressure, and other health issues. And you know what many of those problems trace back to? Years of partying and neglecting their health.

There's nothing wrong with celebrating, but partying should be about celebrating wins, not drowning your problems in alcohol. I learned that lesson early when I was working at a club at 21. The flashy people wearing Gucci and Versace rarely tipped because they usually didn't have much money left. As a bartender, I quickly learned to watch for the regular guys who came in wearing simple clothes with no jewelry. They were often the ones who tipped the most.

Life is funny like that. It's full of opposites. The things that truly matter usually aren't material possessions. What really matters is doing the small things right and building a foundation of discipline and consistency.

## The Ripple Effect of Small Mistakes

Let me share something with you, my friend. Small mistakes can create a ripple effect that spreads far beyond the moment they occur. It's like throwing a pebble into a pond. The ripples expand outward and affect everything around them. The same principle applies to the small mistakes we make in our lives.

I remember a time when I forgot to check the expiration date on my passport before a business trip. It seemed like a small oversight, but it triggered a chain of problems. I was denied entry into the country I was visiting, had to book a last-minute flight back home, and ended up paying extra for rebooking and rescheduling everything. It was a stressful situation that could have been avoided if I had paid attention to that one small detail.

Small mistakes can also affect our relationships in powerful ways. A careless word or thoughtless action can hurt someone we care about. Even if we apologize and try to make things right, the impact may linger. Trust is fragile, and once it is damaged, rebuilding it takes time and effort. It's important to remember that our words and actions, no matter how small they seem, can leave a lasting impression on the people around us.

At the same time, small actions can create positive ripples in our lives. Taking a moment to show appreciation to a colleague, helping a friend in need, or contributing to a charitable cause may seem minor, but those actions can mean a great deal to someone else. Acts of kindness and generosity often spread outward, inspiring others to do the same and creating a chain reaction of goodwill.

In fact, it's often the small actions that lay the foundation for success in every area of life. Whether it's in your career, your relationships, or your personal growth, the consistent practice of small habits can lead to meaningful results over time. It's the daily commitment to discipline, learning, and self-improvement that sets people apart and helps them achieve their goals.

So, my friend, don't underestimate the power of small actions. Pay attention to the details, make conscious choices, and cultivate positive habits. Remember that every decision, no matter how small it may seem, has the potential to create a ripple effect that shapes your future. Build a strong foundation through consistent actions, and you'll see how those habits compound and move you toward a life of fulfillment and achievement.

Keep pushing forward, my friend, and never underestimate the impact of the small actions you take every day.

# CHAPTER 12
## Vibration

Have you ever noticed how conversations with some people flow effortlessly, while with others it feels like you're constantly interrupting each other? This phenomenon can be explained through the idea of vibration, an important element of our existence. Everything on Earth operates through waves, and much like music, these vibrations can either harmonize or clash. When we engage in conversation, our energy can align with someone else's or create disruption. A conversation that flows naturally often suggests that two people are operating at similar frequencies, while constant interruptions may signal a mismatch in energy.

Vibration is universal and influences many of our interactions. Music provides a powerful analogy. Elements such as bass, treble, and octaves exist at specific wavelengths that allow them to blend together in harmony. When they are balanced correctly, the result is a unified and pleasing sound. When they interfere with one another, however, the result becomes unpleasant noise. Life often works in a similar way. When you project positive energy, you tend to attract people, experiences, and opportunities that resonate with that same energy. This helps explain why individuals who carry a sense of motivation and optimism often experience greater success in different areas of life, including financial success. Their positive outlook tends to attract favorable circumstances, a concept often associated with the law of attraction.

On the other hand, individuals who dwell in negativity often attract misfortune and sadness, creating a cycle that reinforces despair. Their outlook and choices generate a lower emotional frequency that tends to repel positivity. This connection between vibration and life experiences can be compared to a calm pond. When the water is still, it reflects peace and clarity. However, throwing a rock into the pond creates ripples that disturb the calm, much like overthinking or unnecessary drama can disturb our inner peace. Those ripples spread throughout the pond, just as our emotional reactions can affect the environment around us. For this reason, it is important to practice responding rather than reacting. By pausing to observe our feelings and responding thoughtfully to situations, we can create more positive ripples in our lives.

When we operate at a higher emotional frequency, we tend to attract people and opportunities that align with that energy. Most people have experienced the discomfort of being around someone who gives off what we commonly call "bad vibes." This feeling often appears without a clear logical explanation. It simply reflects an intuitive recognition that their energy doesn't align with yours. People who operate at lower emotional frequencies often gravitate toward each other, creating environments that can feel negative or toxic. If you ever find yourself wondering why certain people irritate you, it may be because your energies are simply not aligned.

Surrounding yourself with high-vibrational individuals can significantly elevate your own energy. Positive and uplifting friends encourage growth and support your goals, while people who dwell in negativity can pull you down. The old saying that you become the average of the five people you spend the most time with holds a great deal of truth. When you associate with individuals who uplift and inspire you, it becomes easier to grow and reach higher levels of fulfillment.

Reflecting on personal experiences can make this idea clearer. I once had a close friend with whom I shared a bond built mostly around our mutual love for drinking. Over time, I noticed that my life became increasingly negative whenever I spent time with him. Arrests and blackouts started becoming common occurrences.

Eventually, I recognized the pattern and decided to distance myself for a couple of years so I could focus on personal growth.

Even though our friendship still existed, I found that every phone call would eventually turn into an argument because he tried to pull me back into the same lifestyle. I realized that stepping away was not a reflection of how I felt about him. It was simply a necessary decision for my own well-being.

Love embodies the highest vibration, an energy that rises above all others. When you experience love, whether romantic, platonic, or familial, you connect at one of the most elevated emotional frequencies possible. Many people view this energy as closely connected to the divine, representing the highest form of positivity and fulfillment. In contrast, hate resonates at the lowest frequency, often creating chaos and conflict in our lives and in the world around us. Many of the struggles we see today stem from a collective tendency to embrace anger and resentment rather than the more difficult, yet more rewarding, path of love.

Ultimately, choosing love and cultivating higher emotional vibrations can enrich our lives and contribute to a more peaceful existence. Like the still waters of a well-tended pond, love brings clarity and calm that allow us to grow and thrive. As we move through life, we should strive to elevate our energy, attract positivity, and build connections that uplift and inspire. In the end, it is this commitment to love that can guide us toward a brighter and more harmonious future.

# CHAPTER 13
## The Law Of Lust And Love

In exploring the complex relationship between lust and love, or more directly, sex and love, it becomes clear that these two ideas, while often connected, represent very different aspects of human experience. A conversation I once had with a friend highlighted this distinction clearly. He boldly claimed that the most important thing in life is "pussy." His blunt honesty, although shocking at first, opened the door to a deeper conversation about the motivations behind human behavior. He argued that the pursuit of sex drives men to work harder, provide resources, buy nice things, and shape their lives around this single goal. Curious about his perspective, I asked him to explain further. As he continued, it became clear that he was confusing lust with love.

When I told him that love, not lust, holds the greater importance in life, he challenged my view. He insisted that his desire for sex was simply another form of love. I disagreed and explained that the two are not the same. Love represents something deeper and more meaningful. Many people describe it as a divine force, something connected to God and the foundation of true human connection and fulfillment. This led us to discuss the biblical story of Adam and Eve. My friend argued that God created Eve primarily to satisfy Adam's physical desires. I countered that the true purpose was companionship rather than mere physical pleasure. It served as a reminder that giving in to base desires can lead people astray, much like Adam choosing to follow temptation rather than wisdom.

The distinction between lust and love is profound. Lust is a physical urge that is often fleeting and difficult to satisfy, while love exists on a deeper level and creates a connection that goes beyond the physical. Sexual encounters can eventually become routine, but love can remain a lasting source of joy, growth, and meaning.

I asked my friend a hypothetical question. If his wife were to lose her physical beauty or certain physical qualities, would he still love her? He answered yes. That response revealed something important. His feelings were rooted in love rather than lust. This realization highlights the true nature of meaningful relationships. Love is the foundation on which lasting connections are built.

Men, in particular, are often driven by a sense of purpose that goes beyond temporary pleasure. A man's mission in life should involve growth, development, and the pursuit of relationships that align with his values and goals. Unfortunately, distractions, especially those connected to sexual desire, can easily pull a man away from that path. It's important for a man to recognize when a relationship becomes a distraction and to step back, refocus, and seek companions who support his long-term vision.

While sex is certainly an enjoyable part of life, history shows that it has also played a role in many conflicts and tragedies. Stories like *The Iliad* and *The Odyssey* remind us that unchecked desire can lead to chaos and destruction. The lesson is not that sexual connection should be ignored, but that it should never overshadow the value of the individual. True intimacy grows from understanding and appreciating someone as a complete person, not simply focusing on physical attraction.

Human nature often inclines us to desire what remains out of reach. Such longing can distort our perceptions, making lust appear not merely as a desire but as a necessity. My friend's fixation on sex reflected a deeper sense of deprivation, a yearning that clouded his understanding of what love truly is. Yet once a person has experienced sufficient physical intimacy, the limitations of lust become more apparent, and the need for deeper emotional and spiritual connections begins to emerge. Lust, by its nature, can become a distraction from these deeper bonds. For this reason, traditional teachings, particularly those found in the Bible, emphasize the value of waiting for marriage. When sexual relationships develop without a foundation of genuine love, they often give rise to manipulation, disillusionment, and deeper struggles with self-worth.

Ultimately, learning to love both oneself and others cultivates a sense of purpose that lust alone can never provide. Love nurtures motivation and direction in life, much like a sense of divine purpose guiding each individual's path. As we navigate the complexities of human relationships, it becomes essential to distinguish between lust and love and to embrace the latter as the truer source of fulfillment. Such understanding not only enriches our lives but also aligns us with a higher sense of meaning, fostering connections that resonate with depth, sincerity, and lasting significance.

# CHAPTER 14

## Men Don't Cry

In the world of men, there is an unspoken rule: don't cry. But when I say "man, don't cry," I mean it metaphorically. Of course, it's okay to be human, to shed a tear, to be vulnerable, and sometimes to share your emotions with others. We all do this. But leave the crying to the women. When a woman cries, the world takes notice. Her emotions often shape how others perceive her, and she may be seen as incapable of rational thought. But when men cry, the world doesn't seem to care about our emotions or about what someone has done to us. A man is expected to take control of his own destiny.

So when I say "don't cry," I mean it metaphorically. Complaining only prolongs misery. Think about it. The last time you complained about something, did it make the situation better? Of course it didn't. More often, it only makes things worse. Complaining can become a disease that festers in the confines of the human mind. Sometimes it can even feel comforting to wallow in our own misery with others. But as men, we must set aside our complaints and emotions and think rationally. If we're going to solve our problems, we need a clear mind and a calm approach.

Think of emotions as the ocean. When a hurricane or powerful storm hits, the ocean becomes violent and destructive, capable of devastating entire civilizations. But when the ocean is calm and steady, life thrives within it and continues to create more life. In the same way, when a man becomes consumed by complaint or emotional turmoil, progress can come to a halt. We must learn that not everything is as serious as it seems. We should focus on what's in front of us and control only what we can, leaving the rest to a higher power.

A crying man, a man who can't control his emotions, is not truly a man. A man sees things for what they are. He doesn't let a woman or anyone else manipulate him emotionally to the point where he loses control. A real man walks away from unnecessary conflicts. A man can't allow another man to dictate how he feels, because that gives control to someone else. A real man controls himself within so that he can create without.

I've witnessed men who let everything get to them. They were stressed at work, their women stressed them about money, and they argued with everyone who disagreed with them. These men didn't get very far and eventually ended up in mental institutions, relying on others to help manage their emotions. This is why it's crucial for a man to have healthy ways of dealing with stress. We are not like women. Women tend to internalize their emotions and act accordingly. As men, we are external creatures. We create from our minds. One thing a man can't do is let the world dictate how he feels. A man must have perspective, because it gives light to new life. By understanding how the world works, a negative can become a positive and a positive can become a negative. Through rational thinking, we learn how to lead, endure, and remain strong. This is why, in my opinion, men make better leaders.

Think about it. How many women have been presidents? I'm not necessarily biased against the idea of a woman becoming president, but who would you rather have pressing that button? A man who can rationalize and maintain perspective, or someone who lets their emotions get the best of them? Men have an uncanny ability to set their feelings aside for the greater good. Women often have a harder time doing this, largely because they were raised to believe they were delicate, beautiful, and little angels. A man, on the other hand, was taught that he is strong, athletic, and capable of conquering the world. This is why there is confusion in the world today. Many men are raised primarily by women and have become more emotionally driven. That is why you see a rise in feminism and men who are more focused on their appearance. They are often called "pretty boys," striving to impress women and the world.

But a real man wears what he needs, has who he is meant to have, and possesses just enough to fulfill himself. A man raised by his father often grows up emotionally secure because he is taught that the world is a dangerous place and that caution must be exercised. A father teaches his son the ways of survival and the importance of family. A woman, on the other hand, teaches a man about security and the ability to be nourished and cared for.

So my advice to you is simple: suck it up. No one is going to save you. You must save yourself. The idea of being saved belongs more to the stories told to women, the damsel in distress waiting to be rescued. The stories we hear as children, where princesses are saved and kissed by princes and then live happily ever after, are stories meant for women. For a man, life is about falling and getting back up. It is about finding that source of strength, using it, and transforming misery into prosperity.

# CHAPTER 15
## The Law Of Discipline

Discipline is often misunderstood and frequently tangled with the concept of consistency. While both are crucial for personal growth and success, they serve different functions. Discipline is your personal law. It represents the rules you set for yourself, while consistency is the act of adhering to those rules time and time again. To thrive in this world, establishing a solid foundation of discipline is essential.

**Understanding Discipline**

Discipline is akin to the framework of a house. It is the concrete slab upon which everything else is built. Without it, you risk constructing a life that lacks stability and purpose. Think about it. Discipline means doing the things you don't necessarily want to do, but doing them with a commitment that eventually transforms those actions into acts of love.

For instance, consider martial artists or MMA fighters. Their discipline involves rigorous training routines that they follow consistently. They don't just spar or train when they feel like it. Training becomes a lifestyle. Through years of practice, their movements become second nature. Muscle memory allows them to perform under pressure without hesitation.

**The Power of Routine**

The beauty of discipline lies in its ability to create patterns in our lives. Imagine waking up early, eating a healthy breakfast, going to the gym, and tackling your workday. Over time, these actions become ingrained in your routine. At first, any new endeavor feels daunting. I don't care if it's as simple as tying your shoes. The first few attempts can feel awkward. But with repetition, those awkward moments transform into fluidity.

Discipline is your friend, but it also acts as a parental figure in your life. You must learn to parent yourself, making decisions that align with your goals rather than indulging in fleeting desires.

## The Temptation of Instant Gratification

We live in a world filled with distractions and temptations. It's easy to fantasize about jetting off to Jamaica, partying on a yacht, and sipping champagne while surrounded by beautiful people. But if you indulged every whim, you'd likely find yourself far from your goals.

Instead, discipline requires you to prioritize long-term satisfaction over short-term pleasure. It's about creating laws for yourself, personal guidelines that direct your actions toward achieving your aspirations. The exciting part is that you can tailor these laws to fit your unique life journey.

## Crafting Your Ideal Self

Think of it like playing a video game where you get to create your character. If you had the chance to design a person from scratch, how would you envision them? Would you want them to languish on the couch, mindlessly consuming junk food and binge-watching television shows? Probably not. You'd want that character to be dynamic and driven, someone who makes money, drives an impressive car, and lives in a thriving environment.

This idea of creating your ideal self is crucial. It encourages you to actively participate in your own life rather than simply drifting through it. Many people just try to get by, but that's not how you win at life. You need to approach life as a game where the objective is to grow and evolve.

## The Road to Mastery

Discipline is not merely a tool; it's a lifestyle choice. As you cultivate discipline, you'll find that it lays the groundwork for other essential skills such as resilience, focus, and perseverance. Here is how you can build that discipline into your life:

1.  **Set Clear Goals**: Know what you want to achieve. Break your larger goals into smaller, manageable tasks that you can tackle daily.

2.  **Establish Routines**: Create daily habits that align with your goals. Morning routines, work schedules, and evening rituals can all contribute to a disciplined lifestyle.

3.  **Embrace Discomfort**: Understand that growth often occurs outside your comfort zone. Whether it's waking up earlier or pushing through a tough workout, welcome those moments of discomfort as opportunities to grow.

4.  **Track Progress**: Keep a journal or use an app to monitor your achievements. Celebrate small victories along the way, because they can motivate you to keep moving forward.

5.  **Accountability**: Share your goals with a friend or mentor who can hold you accountable. Sometimes knowing that someone else is aware of your progress can strengthen your discipline.

6.  **Learn from Setbacks**: Instead of viewing failures as reasons to give up, see them as valuable lessons. Reflect on what went wrong, adjust your approach, and keep moving forward.

## The Foundation of Success

Discipline is the bedrock of success. Without it, you lack the foundation needed to build your dreams. Imagine trying to construct a house without laying the groundwork first. It would collapse under its own weight. In the same way, without discipline, your aspirations can crumble when faced with challenges.

When you commit to discipline, you're not simply following rules. You're creating a framework for a fulfilling life. You're making a promise to yourself to strive for greatness, even when the path becomes difficult.

**Final Thoughts: Winning the Game of Life**

Discipline is one of the most significant themes explored in this chapter because it shapes your character and ultimately determines your success. Life is not merely about existing; it's about winning the game. You have the power to craft your narrative and create the version of yourself you aspire to become.

So take a moment to reflect. If you were designing your ideal life, what would it look like? What actions would you take each day to turn that vision into reality? Embrace discipline as your guiding principle, and you'll find that the life you want is not just a dream but an achievable reality.

In the end, the law of discipline is not simply a concept. It's a way of life. It's about committing to your growth and taking deliberate steps to manifest your dreams. The journey may be challenging, but the rewards are immeasurable. Choose discipline and watch as you transform your life into a masterpiece.

# CHAPTER 16
## The Law Of Consistency

L et's dive into a crucial element of success: **consistency**. We've already laid the groundwork with discipline, your personal laws. Consistency is how you carry out those laws. Think of it as the steady drumbeat in your life, the metronome that keeps you on track. It means doing the same thing time and again, like a squirrel hoarding nuts for winter.

**The Compounding Effect**

Consistency is powerful; it creates a compounding effect. The small, seemingly insignificant actions you take each day can add up to monumental accomplishments. Take my journey of writing this book, for instance. When I first started, it felt like a Mount Everest-sized climb, and I was just a tiny ant trying to ferry a crumb.

So what did I do? I established a simple discipline: write two chapters every weekend. I wasn't in a rush; I knew that if I stuck to this plan, those chapters would eventually accumulate. And lo and behold, here I am, holding a hefty book that feels more like a therapy session than a literary masterpiece.

Even if I missed a weekend or two, no biggie. I simply doubled up the following weekend, cramming like a student before finals. Consistency doesn't just build a path; it constructs a highway to success.

## The Myth of Instant Mastery

Now, let's clear up a common misconception: people often say, "I've been doing this for ages and I'm still not good at it." Yet you rarely hear that from someone who practices consistently. If you keep working, you will improve. You could even become an astronaut if you truly commit. Sure, you will need to master rocket science and space travel, but steady study will take you there.

Want to become the next Michael Jordan or Tom Brady? Consistency is your ticket. The secret is to repeat a skill until you succeed, then repeat it again just for the joy of mastery.

## The Hidden Work

We idolize our favorite musicians, actors, and athletes, but we rarely witness the effort they invest offstage. What happens in the dark eventually comes to light, so those late-night practice sessions and early-morning workouts are part of the grand plan.

Picture a seed buried underground. No one sees it, yet it grows roots and prepares to sprout. Consistency is doing what you need to do when no one is watching, like choosing a kale salad while your friends enjoy pizza.

## The Arena of Life

Imagine yourself in an empty arena. You are out there honing your craft with no audience to applaud, but one day that arena will be filled with fans cheering your name.

Consistency and discipline are the dynamic duo of success, the Batman and Robin of your personal journey. Put them together and you have a formula for achievement. Now, let's flip the coin for a moment.

## The Flip Side of Consistency

If you consistently make unwise choices (for example, binge-watching reality TV every night or scrolling through your phone instead of going to the gym), you will still get results—just not the ones you want.

Think of it this way: if your idea of "discipline" is endless scrolling on TikTok instead of studying, your grades will mirror that commitment. As the old saying goes, you reap what you sow, and if you are sowing seeds of procrastination, be ready for a harvest of regret.

## Finding Balance

To stay on track, be mindful of what you do repeatedly. Ask yourself, "Does this action align with my goals, or am I simply spinning my wheels?"

Here is a secret: you can design a disciplined routine that makes even the mundane enjoyable. Turn everyday tasks into a personal challenge. Can you finish your workout while dancing to your favorite music? Can you draft those two chapters with the enthusiasm of a child pleading for extra bedtime?

## Conclusion: The Path to Success

In the grand scheme of life, consistency is your closest ally, guiding you steadily through the chaos. Whether you are writing a book, mastering a sport, or striving to become a better version of yourself, remember that every small effort matters.

So, as you move forward, keep the beat steady. Dance to your own rhythm and do not hesitate to make some noise. With discipline and consistency, you will reach the finish line in style, surrounded by a cheering crowd.

Now go, be deliberate in your pursuits, and stay consistent. You have got this!

# CHAPTER 17
## The Law Of Heaven And Hell

When it comes to the afterlife, many people accept a time-honored narrative: upon death you either rise to a heavenly realm, complete with angels, clouds, and an endless supply of milk and honey, or you descend into a fiery abyss of eternal torment. Yet the truth is simple: no one really knows what awaits us once we leave this mortal coil.

Thought for a couple of seconds

**The Great Unknown**

No one has ever returned from the dead to give a detailed account of the afterlife. Despite countless books, documentaries, and religious teachings, the truth remains elusive. Are we greeted by heavenly hosts, or do we simply cease to exist? For now, the answer is hidden from us.

One insight does emerge from this maze of beliefs: heaven and hell are not just destinations; they are perspectives that shape our time on Earth.

**Heaven on Earth**

Consider what heaven feels like. Rather than a distant paradise, it is a state of being. When you are in a heavenly frame of mind, you feel grounded and secure. You wake up with purpose, emotional balance, and genuine appreciation for life. You look around and see beauty everywhere. Love surrounds you—family, friends, and even the neighbor who returns your lawn mower.

This well-being is not produced by your surroundings but by your inner life. You can inhabit chaos and still find heaven within. Emotional stability helps you cultivate joy, gratitude, and a deep sense of fulfillment; these feelings are the foundation of a heavenly existence.

Practicing gratitude lets you collect positive moments. You begin to notice small delights: a warm cup of coffee in the morning, a child's laughter, or a sunset that takes your breath away. Heaven becomes less a physical location and more an emotional state.

**The Path to Accumulated Joy**

To live in this state of heaven, you must actively nurture it. This involves several key practices:

1. **Gratitude**: Start each day by listing the things you are grateful for. This simple act can shift your perspective from lack to abundance.

2. **Mindfulness**: Practice being present. Whether during a meal or in a conversation, being fully engaged can deepen your appreciation for life.

3. **Positive Relationships**: Surround yourself with uplifting individuals. The company you keep can significantly influence your emotional state.

4. **Self-Care**: Prioritize your mental and physical health. Engage in activities that promote well-being, whether through exercise, reading, or pursuing a hobby.

5. **Service to Others**: Helping others can create a ripple effect of positivity in your life. When you contribute to the happiness of others, you often find your own joy magnified.

**The Hell Within**

On the flip side of this coin lies the concept of hell. While heaven is characterized by positivity and joy, hell is often a manifestation of negativity and despair. Those who dwell in this state may find themselves trapped in a cycle of self-destructive behavior, filled with bitterness, resentment, and hopelessness.

Living in this mental and emotional hell can lead to devastating outcomes. People may resort to harmful coping mechanisms, such as substance abuse or self-harm, as they struggle to escape their inner turmoil. This negativity often manifests in their relationships, causing them to gossip, judge others, and lash out.

When you allow negativity to dominate your life, you create a self-fulfilling prophecy. You attract more negativity, perpetuating a cycle that feels inescapable. This is why some individuals reach a breaking point, feeling as though they have descended into their own personal hell.

## The Power of Perspective

The key takeaway is that perspective shapes your reality. Each morning presents a new opportunity to choose your mindset. You can wake up and choose gratitude, or you can allow the weight of the world to dictate your mood.

**Gratitude vs. Resentment**: Think about it. Some people rise with a sense of purpose and are grateful for another day to make an impact. Others wake up wishing they could pull the covers over their heads, consumed by dread and resentment.

Life can be brutal, and it can certainly throw challenges your way. However, your response to those challenges is what ultimately defines your experience. You have the power to choose whether to let life beat you down or to rise above it.

## Taking Ownership

Too often, people blame external factors for their dissatisfaction. "I'm not where I'm supposed to be because of my job," or "I can't find happiness because of my relationships."

However, the reality is that you are the architect of your own life. Your thoughts, feelings, and actions shape your reality.

When you take ownership of your circumstances, you can begin to shift your perspective. This doesn't mean ignoring hardships. Instead, it means acknowledging them and choosing to respond in a way that aligns with your desired state of being.

**The Duality of Existence**

Heaven and hell are two sides of the same coin. While they may seem like opposites, they are intrinsically linked. Recognizing this duality can empower you to navigate life's ups and downs more effectively.

- **Emotional Resilience**: Cultivating resilience allows you to face challenges without succumbing to despair. You can experience setbacks without letting them define you.

- **Awareness of Choice**: Understanding that you have the power to choose your perspective can be liberating. It places the responsibility for your happiness squarely in your hands.

- **Empathy and Compassion**: Recognizing that others may also be trapped in their own hell can foster empathy. This understanding can improve your relationships and help create a more supportive environment.

**Conclusion: Choose Your Reality**

Ultimately, the law of heaven and hell teaches us that where you dwell, both mentally and emotionally, is a choice. You can cultivate a life filled with joy, gratitude, and peace, or you can allow negativity and despair to take root.

As you navigate your journey, remember that perspective is key. Choose to wake up each day with gratitude and intention. Embrace the opportunities before you and strive to create your own version of heaven on earth.

So, which reality will you choose today? The power lies within you.

# CHAPTER 18
## The Illusion Of Control

*(Control yourself, and let go of what you cannot)*

———————◆———————

In the vast tapestry of life, there exists a profound truth: control is but an illusion. We are often driven by the desire to control people, circumstances, and even the unpredictable nature of life itself. However, the reality is that we can only control our own actions and choices. Everything else must be released into the ether and surrendered to the flow of the universe.

In this journey called life, there are countless unknowns that lie beyond our grasp. We cannot predict the future, for we are not fortunetellers. Our only solace lies in the realm of probability. If we bounce a ball, the probability that it will rise and fall is certain. If we drink water, the probability of hydration is certain. And if we were to fall from a towering building, the probability of death is certain. It is these probabilities that should guide us in our pursuit of control.

Consider the aspiring athlete who dreams of reaching the heights of professional sports. The probability of making it to the NFL, NBA, or Major League Baseball may seem slim. Yet within this realm of uncertainty lies the power to shape one's own destiny. Through dedication, hard work, and relentless perseverance, an athlete can increase the probability of success. The same principle applies to any goal or aspiration in life. You can become what you desire, but only if you are willing to put in the work.

The path to success is paved with failures, setbacks, and moments of doubt. Those who have achieved their dreams have often failed countless times before their breakthrough. It is in those moments of despair that true strength is forged. Just like the characters in the Bible who endured many trials and tribulations, we too must embrace our own journey of growth and transformation.

God has a way of breaking us down, teaching us valuable lessons, and ultimately making us whole again. He challenges us to become stronger, wiser, and more resilient. If we seek strength, he presents us with challenges that test our limits. If we yearn for wealth, he shows us what it means to be poor. If we desire love, he reveals the complexities of human relationships. It is the yin and yang of life, the interplay of light and darkness that shapes us.

Amid these challenges, the key to maintaining our equilibrium lies in understanding what we can control and what we cannot. In my own life, I reflect on my past marriage. Communication issues and a struggle for control ultimately led to our downfall. We failed to realize that true growth comes from controlling ourselves rather than attempting to change others. We can only control our own actions, not the actions of those around us.

When faced with financial struggles, illness, or the consequences of our own mistakes, we must focus on what we can control. We can manage our spending habits, prioritize our needs, and create budgets to reduce debt. We can choose to nourish our bodies with healthy foods and engage in physical activity to support our recovery. And when worry consumes our thoughts, we must remember that it is a manifestation of fear. Worrying about the outcomes of situations is futile, similar to trying to unravel the mysteries of the universe. We must let go and trust that everything will work out in the end.

We cannot control external circumstances or the actions of others. Each individual's journey is intertwined with the collective tapestry of humanity. All we can do is control our own actions and strive for the best possible outcome. Stress and misery are born from the futile desire to control what is beyond our grasp. We must relinquish this burden and embrace the magic of letting go, trusting in a higher power to guide us.

God will never bestow upon us more than we are ready to handle. He knows that true growth and understanding come from experiencing the journey and learning how to use the blessings we receive. If everything we desired were granted to us without effort, we would not appreciate its value. We must go through the necessary steps, endure hardships, and learn from the challenges that come our way.

In this process, it is vital to remember that comparing ourselves to others is futile. Each of us has a unique path, and what is meant for someone else may not be meant for us. God wants us to control ourselves so that we can work through Him to provide what is needed to help others in this troubled world.

So, my advice to you, dear reader, is this: if uncertainty looms over your future, let go and let God. Control what you can control, but have the wisdom to recognize what lies beyond your reach. Embrace the journey, endure the challenges, and trust that everything will work out in the end. Meet God halfway by disciplining yourself and preparing for the blessings that await you.

Remember, control is an illusion, but the power to shape your own destiny lies within. Let go of the need for control.

# CHAPTER 19

## Just Do It

———◆———

Nike's slogan, "Just Do It," is a simple yet profound mantra that resonates deeply with the complexity of life. In a world where we often overthink and hesitate, those three words serve as a powerful reminder that action is the key to progress. Life can feel like a labyrinth of uncertainties, but when you strip it down, it really comes down to one simple truth: **just do it**.

### The Weight of Procrastination

Procrastination is the thief of time, and let's face it, time is the one resource we can never reclaim. Think about how easy it is to spend hours scrolling through social media or binge-watching a show, only to realize those hours could've been spent pursuing something meaningful. Too often, we let the fear of failure paralyze us, trapping us in an endless cycle of "what ifs." But what if you shifted your focus? Instead of worrying about what might go wrong, what if you focused on what could go right?

The truth is that not every attempt will lead to success, and that's okay. Trying is what leads to growth. Someone once asked me what the meaning of life is, and after reflecting on it, I realized it comes down to *creation*. Life is a canvas. If you're not creating something with it, you might as well be watching paint dry.

### Creating Your Reality

When you step back and look at the bigger picture, the universe itself is a grand act of creation. Just like the cosmos, we're all capable of creating in our own way. Whether it's a piece of art, a business, a relationship, or even a simple meal, creation always requires action. Inspiration rarely appears out of thin air. You have to get up, roll up your sleeves, and **just do it**.

Many people fail to recognize how small, consistent actions accumulate into meaningful achievements. You can't expect to build your dream life while lounging on the couch, snack in hand, watching cat videos. The comforts we enjoy today exist because of the hard work and sacrifices made by those who came before us. They didn't sit around waiting for life to happen. They worked, struggled, and pushed forward because they believed their efforts mattered.

## The Power of Action

The phrase "just do it" is powerful because it guarantees movement. Even if your first attempt fails, you've still made progress, and progress always leads to learning. Not every dream will come true, but every effort moves you closer to discovering your true path. If you ever find yourself stuck in a rut, repeat those three words: **just do it**.

Think about the tasks you've been putting off. Maybe it's finishing an important project, getting in shape, or finally taking control of your finances. Whatever it is, taking action can change the trajectory of your life. Sometimes the hardest part is simply starting.

And let's not forget the habits that hold us back. Sometimes "just do it" means choosing not to do something at all. If you struggle with addiction, saying no to that drink or resisting that temptation can be just as powerful as taking action. Discipline, after all, is action in the form of restraint.

## The Laziness Trap

Ah, laziness. The silent killer of dreams. If laziness had a face, it would probably be grinning from ear to ear, knowing it has quietly derailed countless ambitions. Left unchecked, laziness doesn't stay small. It grows, feeding on comfort and routine until inaction becomes a habit.

In fact, you could argue that laziness deserves a place among the greatest warnings humanity has ever given itself. Imagine if it had made its way into the Ten Commandments: "Thou shalt not be lazy." The idea may sound humorous, but the truth behind it is serious. Laziness breeds more laziness, and before long, you find yourself trapped in a cycle where dreams fade and opportunities pass by.

People often criticize the wealthy, assuming their success is rooted in greed. But more often than not, the difference comes down to action. They took risks, made decisions, and pushed forward when others hesitated. Talking about your dreams is free. Taking action costs time, effort, and energy, but that is the price of progress, and it's a price worth paying.

**The Cost of Inaction**

If you want to achieve anything meaningful, you must be willing to sacrifice your time and energy. It's a simple equation: effort produces results. Nothing worth having comes easy, and when you find yourself procrastinating, remember that you're not just wasting time. You're wasting life itself.

Every moment spent delaying what matters most is a moment you'll never get back. Progress requires movement, and movement requires effort.

When the urge to procrastinate creeps in, remind yourself of those three simple words: **just do it**. Whether it's waking up early, tackling a project you've been avoiding, or getting your life back in order, action is the antidote to stagnation.

**The Dangers of Overthinking**

Overthinking has a way of trapping us in our own minds. It's like standing at the edge of a diving board, debating whether to jump. The longer you stand there, the more fear builds until you feel frozen in place.

At some point, you have to stop analyzing and take the plunge. Act first. Adjust as you go.

Have you ever noticed how some people are all talk and no action? They'll tell you about their grand plans and the amazing things they're going to accomplish. But when the moment arrives to follow through, they disappear.

If I had a dime for every time I heard someone say, "I'm going to do this," only to watch nothing happen, I'd be a millionaire by now.

**The Art of Follow-Through**

Starting something is important, but finishing it is where real progress happens. Anyone can dream. Not everyone follows through.

Sometimes it's better to take the first step before you have everything figured out. Clarity often comes through action, not endless planning. What matters most is that once you start, you commit to seeing it through.

The difference between a dreamer and a doer is simple: the doer takes action and keeps going.

So the next time you find yourself caught in the web of procrastination, stop, take a breath, and repeat those three words: **just do it**. Whether you're tackling a project, confronting a challenge, or breaking a bad habit, remember that every journey begins with a single step.

Get up. Get moving. **Just do it.**

Life is waiting for you to take action.

# CHAPTER 20

## If You Never Start, You Can Never Finish

*The Power of Starting: A Journey to Accomplishment*

**Introduction**

My father taught me a simple lesson: *If you never start, you can never finish.*

Have you ever found yourself constantly dreaming about achieving great things, only to realize that you never actually take the steps needed to turn those dreams into reality? It's a common struggle for many of us. Too often, we give in to the fear of failure or the fear of the unknown.

But here's the hard truth: if we never start, we'll never finish.

In this chapter, I want to share some of my personal experiences and insights about the importance of taking action and how it can profoundly impact our lives.

**The Invention That Never Was**

Let me take you back to a time when I was just seven years old, filled with youthful enthusiasm and boundless imagination. During that period, I came up with what I thought was an ingenious invention called "Talk and Type." The idea was simple but revolutionary: a computer program that could transcribe spoken words into written text.

As a child, I despised writing and wished there was a way to make it easier. I imagined a system where you could simply speak and have your words appear instantly on the page. At the time, it felt like a brilliant solution to a problem I faced every day.

Little did I know that years later this very idea would become a reality through speech recognition technology.

Yet despite having this idea at such a young age, I never took any steps to bring it to life. Instead, I shared the idea with friends and family, hoping someone might recognize its potential.

Looking back, I sometimes wonder if one of those people ever pursued the idea and turned it into something successful. I'll probably never know.

What I do know is that the experience taught me an important lesson. An idea by itself isn't enough. Without action, even the most creative ideas remain nothing more than thoughts.

That missed opportunity opened my eyes to the importance of seizing the moment and taking action.

## Responsibilities and Choices

As we grow older, life presents us with an ever-increasing list of responsibilities and obligations. Whether it's paying bills, maintaining healthy relationships, or fulfilling our duties as parents, the demands on our time and energy can feel overwhelming.

Men, in particular, often carry a heavy sense of responsibility. We're expected to be providers, protectors, and the glue that holds our families together. While these roles can bring purpose and pride, they can also place a heavy weight on our shoulders. That pressure can leave us feeling exhausted, uncertain, and hesitant to pursue our own dreams and aspirations.

But it's important to remember that life is ultimately shaped by choices and actions. When we avoid making decisions or delay taking action, we're still making a choice. We're allowing circumstances and external forces to decide the direction of our lives.

Real change begins when we take deliberate and intentional steps toward what we want. Only then do we begin to shape our own path and take ownership of our destiny.

## The Importance of Action

Whether we find ourselves pursuing entrepreneurship or simply navigating the challenges of everyday life, action remains the foundation of progress and stability. It doesn't matter whether we work for someone else or build something of our own. What matters most is our willingness to act.

Even when the outcome isn't immediately positive, taking action moves us forward. It teaches us lessons, builds resilience, and helps us discover our strengths. Growth rarely happens through comfort or hesitation. It happens through movement.

Think about someone you know who spends most of their time playing video games or distracting themselves from reality while avoiding their goals and ambitions. If that pattern continues long enough, life begins to move forward without them. Opportunities pass by, responsibilities pile up, and the sense of control over one's own future slowly fades.

To reclaim control of our lives, we must take that first step. Progress begins the moment we decide to act.

## The Journey of Accomplishment

Imagine a life without ambition, without the desire for personal growth, and without the drive to fulfill our responsibilities. At first, it might sound appealing. Many of us fantasize about a life of pure leisure, lounging on a beach and sipping margaritas without a care in the world.

But if we're honest with ourselves, a life without effort would eventually lose its meaning. Without challenges, achievements, and the satisfaction that comes from overcoming obstacles, even the greatest luxuries would begin to feel ordinary.

Life is a tapestry woven with threads of joy, sadness, hardship, love, and hope. Each experience adds depth and meaning to the larger picture. It's through consistent effort and the willingness to take action that we discover purpose and fulfillment.

## Steps to Success

Time, that intangible yet invaluable resource, quietly measures our progress through life. Just as it took time for God to create the Earth, with its vast oceans, towering mountains, and intricate ecosystems, we must also understand that meaningful accomplishments require patience.

Writing this book, for example, has been a journey that has taken two years of steady effort, one page at a time. That patient accumulation of work is what eventually brought the book to life.

Great achievements rarely appear overnight. Monuments are not built in a single day. They're constructed brick by brick and stone by stone. In the same way, every meaningful goal requires patience, persistence, and consistent action.

We must learn to embrace gradual progress and pay attention to the details along the way. Even projects that seem simple on the surface can become surprisingly complex. They demand time, dedication, and perseverance.

But when we commit to taking action and pushing through those complexities, we move closer to achieving the goals that once seemed distant.

## Overcoming Obstacles

Along any meaningful journey, obstacles and setbacks are inevitable. There will be moments when we stumble, fall, and question whether we have what it takes to overcome the challenges before us.

Yet it is during these difficult moments that the power of starting becomes even more important. Instead of allowing setbacks to discourage us, we must learn to see them as opportunities for growth and learning.

Every obstacle gives us a chance to pause, reassess our approach, and refine our strategies. Challenges test our determination, but they also strengthen our character. When we continue to take action in the face of adversity, we develop resilience and the confidence needed to navigate the unpredictable turns of life.

Persistence transforms obstacles into stepping stones, guiding us forward on our journey toward success.

## The Ripple Effect

Taking action does more than change our own lives. It creates a ripple effect that reaches far beyond us.

When we choose to pursue our dreams and take deliberate steps toward our goals, we inspire the people around us. Our actions become a powerful example of what is possible when someone refuses to remain stuck in hesitation.

Courage and determination are contagious. When others see someone working toward their goals, it often sparks a sense of motivation within them. They begin to believe that progress is possible in their own lives as well.

By leading through action, we can encourage others to break free from cycles of doubt and inaction. Our achievements become proof that growth and transformation are within reach for anyone willing to begin the journey.

## Conclusion

The power of starting has the ability to transform both our lives and the lives of those around us. When we choose to act, we unlock our potential, overcome obstacles, and begin moving toward the life we truly want.

Dreams remain distant until we take the first step toward them. Action is what turns possibility into reality.

So I encourage you to embrace the power of starting. Take that first step toward your goals, even if the path ahead feels uncertain. Never underestimate the impact of a single decision to begin.

Greatness often begins with one small act of courage.

Start today and watch as your life unfolds in ways you never thought possible.

**Rules to Live By**

## 1. Breaking the Cycle of Procrastination

Procrastination often holds us back from achieving our goals and dreams. By taking that first step and simply starting, we disrupt the cycle of delay and create momentum. Once we begin, it becomes easier to keep moving forward and build on the progress we've made.

## 2. Building Confidence and Self-Efficacy

Starting is an act of belief in ourselves and in our abilities. Each time we take action and see positive results, our confidence grows. The more we start and accomplish, the more we believe in our capacity to achieve even greater things. Starting becomes a powerful tool for building self-efficacy and strengthening our sense of self-worth.

## 3. Creating Opportunities for Learning and Growth

Starting exposes us to new experiences, challenges, and opportunities for growth. When we take action, we open ourselves to a world of possibilities. Each new endeavor teaches valuable lessons, expands our knowledge, and helps us develop new skills.

## 4.  Overcoming Fear and Resistance

Fear and resistance often accompany the act of starting something new. Yet when we confront these emotions and move through them, we build resilience and develop the strength to overcome obstacles. Starting allows us to face our fears directly and prove to ourselves that we're capable of far more than we once believed.

## 5.  Inspiring Others

When we summon the courage to start and pursue our dreams, we become a source of inspiration for others. Our actions speak louder than words. By taking real steps toward our goals, we encourage those around us to do the same. Our willingness to start can create a ripple effect of positive change within our communities and beyond.

Remember, the power of starting lies within each of us. It's a catalyst for growth, achievement, and personal transformation. Embrace the opportunity to begin, take that first step, and watch as your life unfolds in ways you never thought possible.

### FOR MEN ONLY!!! – *The archetypes of women*

# CHAPTER 21
## Beware Of The Succubus

I gotta tell you, folks, there's something about those succubus types that can really mess with your head. You know, like that episode of *South Park* where Chef, the fun-loving dude, gets his soul sucked out by his girlfriend? Yeah, that's the kind of situation we're talking about here. And let me tell you, it's no joke!

So, what exactly is a succubus? Well, picture this: she comes into your life all beautiful and caring, making you feel like you hit the jackpot. But as time goes on, she starts draining the life out of you, bit by bit. Suddenly, you're buying her everything, doing everything for her, and she's even keeping your kids away from you. It's like she thinks she's the damn prize and you're just there to serve her.

Now, in today's world, we've become infatuated with beauty. I mean, let's be real, we've fallen in love with booty! But here's the thing, fellas: looks fade away. What really matters is personality and soul. Trust me, you don't want to end up with a woman who's all body and no substance. She'll depend on you for everything else, and that's a recipe for disaster.

**Types of Succubus**

**Beware of the Narcissist**

The narcissistic woman is a unique archetype who often remains unaware of her narcissistic tendencies. She possesses an astonishing level of self-absorption, making it difficult for her to see anything beyond herself. These individuals are incredibly selfish, lacking self-awareness and often proving challenging to interact with. Despite claiming intellectual superiority over others, they frequently struggle with self-sufficiency and taking care of themselves independently.

In many ways, they are walking contradictions. They demand admiration, attention, and devotion while failing to live up to the very standards they expect from everyone else. That's the real hypocrisy of it all.

One characteristic of the narcissistic woman is her ability to target and exploit the insecurities of others while remaining completely oblivious to her own. She has a strong desire to see others fail, simply to satisfy her ego and proclaim, "I told you so." This type of woman will gladly let you do all the work for her and then boast to everyone that she accomplished everything on her own. She may even go as far as damaging your property, such as slashing your tires or vandalizing your car, only to later apologize, take you back, and leave you to deal with the costly repairs.

The narcissist is undoubtedly the most dangerous archetype. Her sole focus is on herself, disregarding the well-being of her children, you, and anyone else around her. She is determined to present herself as the smartest, most beautiful, and intellectually superior person anyone has ever encountered. This obsession with self-importance can lead to a toxic and manipulative relationship.

Before long, she will have you spinning in circles in the backyard, engaging in one-sided conversations loud enough to disturb the neighbors. Meanwhile, people in your social circle will be scratching their heads, wondering why you are still with her. To make matters worse, she will slowly begin alienating you from your friends by belittling them and claiming she is superior to them.

The truth is, your friends may not dislike her because they are inferior. They may dislike her simply because she is genuinely unlikeable.

The narcissistic woman has a peculiar ability to project her vulnerabilities and personal issues onto you or your family. In her eyes, she is always right and everyone else is wrong. If multiple people in your life have issues with her, it may be a clear indication that the problem lies with her.

The narcissistic woman refuses to take responsibility for her actions or reactions. Instead, she deflects blame by saying, "They shouldn't have done this to me." Genuine apologies are rarely offered, as she prefers to manipulate situations with outright falsehoods.

It is crucial to stay away from individuals who exhibit narcissistic traits, because they can be incredibly dangerous. Their self-centeredness, obsession with money, and inflated egos make them unpredictable and harmful to those around them. Remember, true growth and self-improvement do not come from religion alone, and using religion as an excuse for selfish or hurtful behavior is unjustifiable. Protect yourself and prioritize your well-being by avoiding these individuals whenever possible.

I once knew a guy who got caught up with the wrong woman. She took everything from him: his soul, his dignity, and his pride. Now he is just a shell of his former self, and it breaks my heart to see it. But he is still with her, and she is sucking the life out of him every single day. It is like watching a slow death.

You see, sometimes we are blind to the signs because we are too close to the situation. That is when you need someone else's perspective. People may warn you, but you brush them off, thinking they are just jealous. But trust me, some people genuinely want to help you. They can see what you cannot see, and that perspective is invaluable.

So let me give you a heads up on some women to avoid: the narcissists. These are the ones who think the world revolves around them. They have no concern for anyone else and believe they are the holy grail of women. Let me tell you, that is not what you want. They should come with a caution sign on their foreheads that says, "I am not what you want."

## Beware of the Damsel in Distress

Alright, guys, let's talk about another archetype that can really mess with your life: the damsel in distress. Now, we have all encountered this type at some point. She is the one who swoops into your life claiming she needs saving from her past relationships and from life in general. And guess what? You are supposed to be her knight in shining armor.

But hold up for a second and take a step back. Have you ever wondered why the other guy left? It is because this damsel cannot do anything for herself. She depends on you for everything. Her light, her dark, her yin, her yang, and pretty much her entire existence. When you become her everything, what is left for you? Not much, my friend.

I get it. It seems innocent at first. You want to be the hero, right? But behind that mask of helplessness is someone who always sees herself as the victim. And let me tell you, being with a victim is no walk in the park. She will blame you for everything that goes wrong in her life. When things get tough, she will push you to the brink of insanity and have you questioning your own sanity.

But here is the kicker. She will take credit for all your accomplishments. Yes, she will claim them as her own and then move on to the next guy with the same mindset. How do I know? Because I have been there, my friend.

I was married to one of these damsels. We were building a life together, and things seemed great, especially compared to her abusive past. But when things started going sour, she accused me of being just like her ex. Can you believe that?

Even though I helped her achieve so many of her dreams, she still found a way to blame me for all her problems. It was like a never-ending cycle of victimhood. And let me tell you, it was frustrating as hell. These damsels will talk about you behind your back, play the victim card to all their friends, and even badmouth you to your own family. Suddenly, you become the villain in their story while they play the hero.

Now, out of all the succubus archetypes, the damsel in distress may seem like the lesser evil. After all, she often doesn't even realize what she is doing to you. Most victims do not, to be honest. They are unable to see that they may be the issue and that they should work on changing themselves instead of constantly pointing fingers. But do not let that fool you, my friend. She may not realize what she is doing, but she is still dangerous.

She will unload all her emotional baggage onto you, making you carry the weight of her past trauma. And trust me, that is a heavy burden to bear. Sure, we all make mistakes in relationships, and I will admit that I was not the perfect husband either. But dealing with someone who constantly plays the victim is a whole different level of difficulty. They have no one else to blame but you, because you are the closest person to them.

Even if you have helped them overcome their fears, insecurities, and hardships, they will still find a way to blame you for any negative outcome, especially if you are not bringing in the big bucks. So, my fellow men, beware of the damsel in distress. Do not let yourself become the scapegoat for someone else's problems.

Remember, you deserve a partner who takes responsibility for their own life and is willing to work on themselves. Do not get caught up in the never-ending cycle of victimhood. Break free, find someone who lifts you up instead of dragging you down, and build a healthy and balanced relationship.

Stay strong, stay aware, and beware of the damsel in distress.

## The Granddaddy Long Legs

The granddaddy long legs is a term used to describe a specific archetype of succubus woman. The name may sound amusing, but it comes from the idea that these women often have unresolved issues with their fathers. Because of a lack of paternal love, they seek out older men who can fill the role of both a father and a lover.

Typically, these women are financially supported by the men they choose to be with, who often end up treating them like daughters. These men shower them with gifts, take them to expensive dinners, and indulge them with extravagant vacations. In many ways, the granddaddy long legs simply wants to be treated in a way she was never treated during her childhood.

It is advisable to stay away from these women, particularly if you are over the age of 50. As a general rule, if a woman is half your age, she could potentially be your daughter. Getting involved with such a woman may leave you stuck with a spoiled, bratty individual who constantly demands material possessions. Unfortunately, this situation can even lead to a premature demise for the older man. Even after death, the granddaddy long legs may still end up claiming everything, since she would likely have been given rights to all of his possessions.

These women can exhibit extreme selfishness. They maintain the appearance of being in a committed relationship while secretly dating men their own age and openly mocking their older partners. They want the freedom to cheat without interference, while proudly showing off the children they have with other men as trophies. Some even wait patiently for the death of their older partners while keeping another man waiting in the wings.

Surprisingly, many older men are willing to tolerate this behavior. They know they cannot match the sexual desires of a younger woman, so they allow the granddaddy long legs to do as she pleases. They convince themselves that these women will never leave and will ultimately take care of them.

While this succubus archetype is dangerous, they are at least somewhat honest about their intentions. They embody the granddaddy long legs archetype, seeking both a father figure and a lover at the same time. It is essential to exercise caution and remain aware of the potential risks associated with becoming involved with someone like this.

## Beware of the Pants Wearer

The Pants Wearer archetype is characterized by a woman who treats her partner like a little boy and assumes a motherly role. It is somewhat similar to the Granddaddy Long Legs archetype, but with a maternal twist. She dictates what he should wear, what he should eat, how to decorate his home, and even how he should interact with others. While this archetype may seem humorous at first, her intention is often to help immature men grow up and become responsible adults. Typically, the men who attract this archetype are those who struggle with maturity and personal growth, often because of choices they have made themselves.

Women who embody the Pants Wearer archetype have usually witnessed this type of dynamic during their own upbringing. Perhaps their fathers were absent, inconsistent, or inadequate providers. As a result, they may have made a conscious decision not to allow a man to control their household or dictate their actions. At the same time, they may still desire companionship and intimacy.

Unfortunately, these women can end up stifling their partner's individuality and passions. While some changes may be necessary for personal growth, it is important for individuals to make their own choices rather than allowing someone else to make those choices for them.

The signs of a Pants Wearer archetype can be subtle. When you first meet them, they may gently encourage their partner to dress in ways that make him appear younger, suggesting outfits or styles that give off a youthful look. They might say things like,

"You look good in a suit. Have you ever tried wearing a fedora?" When you find yourself considering these suggestions, it is important to remember that you should embrace your own preferences and decisions.

While it is perfectly acceptable to let your partner make decisions for you occasionally, it is crucial to maintain your own autonomy. For example, if she suggests having fish for dinner, try switching things up and suggesting steak instead. Do not allow her to control the narrative of your life, because that can eventually lead to her picking out your clothes, dictating your shopping choices, and even influencing your social circle.

In today's society, it is perfectly acceptable for a woman to earn more money than a man. However, it is still important to maintain a sense of balance and avoid allowing her to become the sole provider in the relationship. Find ways to contribute and take on responsibilities that go beyond financial support. When one person controls all the finances, they often end up holding significant power over the other person's actions.

Consider this scenario. If she already makes the money, pays all the bills, and provides all the food, she may feel entitled to assume the role of the dominant partner. Remember, it is important to maintain your own agency and not allow her to become the sole authority figure in your life.

**Beware of the Addict**

The Addict archetype is typically associated with women. You will often encounter them in social settings like bars, pool halls, or clubs. They thrive in these environments and are usually the life of the party. However, as you get to know them better, you begin to realize that the party never ends for them.

They have a tendency to spend money recklessly on things that are unnecessary, such as drugs, alcohol, and constant partying.

Over time, this behavior can lead to financial strain and leave you wondering why the two of you never seem to have enough money.

The Addict archetype may even resort to stealing from you in order to satisfy their addictions. It is also important to understand that addictions are not always related to drugs or alcohol. They can appear in many different forms, such as excessive shopping or constantly watching reality television. The key issue is that when these behaviors are not practiced in moderation, they can eventually lead to serious consequences.

When someone becomes addicted to something, they become consumed by it and struggle to focus on other aspects of life, including their relationships. In many cases, their addiction becomes a higher priority than their love for you. This can drain you both financially and emotionally, leaving you to suffer the consequences.

If you decide to leave them, they may play the victim and claim that you never understood them and that you simply wanted an easy way out. Even if you tried your best to help them grow and change, the healthiest decision for both of you may ultimately be to part ways.

If you truly love someone, you will sometimes have to let them go. People often need to confront and overcome their addictions in order to grow. In some cases, they may even become addicted to you, relying on your understanding and support to sustain them. However, it is important to recognize that nobody can truly understand someone who is wreaking havoc on their own life and the lives of those around them. You can only help someone as much as they are willing to help themselves.

The Addict archetype is characterized by an inability to control addictive tendencies, which often take priority over their relationships. It is wise to stay away from individuals who fall into this archetype unless they have actively worked to overcome their addictions and have developed healthy habits that allow them to prioritize their relationships.

**Beware the Runner**

**The Runner Archetype**

The Runner archetype refers to women who live a fast-paced lifestyle and are always on the move. They are often very attractive and tend to dress in provocative clothing such as short skirts and high heels, wearing these outfits to all kinds of events and gatherings, including barbecues, church, and birthday parties.

This archetype can be particularly dangerous because they constantly attract attention from other men. If you choose to date or enter a relationship with a Runner, you may find yourself in constant competition with other men for her attention.

Men naturally gravitate toward the sexual energy she exudes, which often leads them to approach her and try to manipulate the situation. In some cases, they may even convince her to leave you. Runners are quick to move on from relationships and often look for someone they believe can offer more than you can, whether that means greater financial stability or a more exciting lifestyle. They are also more prone to betrayal and may blame their actions on your supposed lack of attention, even if you have been attentive and supportive.

Dealing with a Runner archetype is like handling a double-edged sword. No matter how you approach it, you are unlikely to come out on top. These women have a strong desire to be desired by men, even as they grow older. You may come across older women who still dress like young girls because they struggle to accept that beauty fades with time and they long for the attention they once received. Many of them remain perpetually single and are always searching for someone new.

It is important to avoid falling into the trap of the Runner archetype. Learn to recognize the signs and remain cautious. While they may be fun, great in bed, and enjoyable to be around, they will often leave you eventually or create significant stress in your life.

If you want to spot this type of woman, you will often find them in clubs, usually in the VIP section. They tend to flaunt material possessions such as jewelry and expensive clothing while projecting an image of wealth and status. However, be prepared for the high level of maintenance that comes with them. Runners love fast cars and often expect their partners to maintain a lifestyle that matches their own self-image as top-tier women.

If you do choose to pursue a relationship with these women, be prepared to have a significant amount of money. If you do not have substantial financial resources, they will likely leave. They are often referred to as the "side chick" because they are typically only interested in being a casual companion and are not reliable for long-term commitments. While they may be fun and carefree, they cannot always be trusted due to their fast-paced lifestyle.

Breaking free from a succubus is not easy. We often make things harder than they need to be because we are afraid the monster will destroy us. In reality, the monster is our fear of being alone and not knowing who we truly are. Sometimes we need to take a step back and discover ourselves before jumping into relationships.

So beware of the succubus, my friends. Do not let them tell you who you are or what you should be doing. It is time to decide that for yourself and find a partner who complements you rather than controls you. Remember, you have to be whole as a person in order to attract another whole person.

Do not let the succubus drain your soul and keep you trapped in a cage. Break free and embrace the journey of self-discovery.

Stay strong, stay true, and beware of the succubus.

# CHAPTER 22
## The Gold Digger Archetype

A h, the infamous gold digger. She is a fascinating character, the kind that makes every man break out in a cold sweat. This woman seems to have it all: beauty, brains, and a hidden agenda. Unlike some other archetypes, she is refreshingly honest about what she wants, and that is your money.

Now let us get one thing straight. A gold digger is not a prostitute. A prostitute exchanges sex for money, while a gold digger exchanges her time. And believe it or not, a gold digger can actually develop feelings for you. How sweet, right?

These women have become accustomed to being spoiled rotten. They expect you to foot the bill, cover their expenses, and shower them with all sorts of material goodies. In many ways, this lifestyle compensates for the lack of attention, intimacy, or self-confidence they may feel they are missing.

The gold digger's role is to make you look like a million bucks and give you instant status among your peers. They have absolutely no shame about what they want. In fact, they will usually tell you the truth about their expectations, which can be refreshing. The problem is that the truth can also make your pockets cry.

They will be upfront about how they plan to take care of you and support your image, but remember that you will likely be paying for their hair, nails, cosmetic procedures, rent, bills, and every other material desire they may have, especially purses and dresses. These women are used to the good life, my friend. They are often drop-dead gorgeous, oozing with confidence, and fiercely independent.

Now here is a word of caution. You need to be careful with a gold digger. Even if you only plan to treat her once or twice, be prepared to break the bank. They usually start with small requests, $100 here and $200 there, until they have drained you of thousands.

If you have enough self-control and do not mind splurging a little, go ahead. Just make it clear that you are not a walking ATM and that the cash withdrawals have a limit. Because if you cannot keep up with the payments, this gold digger will leave you in a heartbeat. She will simply move on to find her next sugar daddy. Loyalty is not her strong suit, my friend. If she is doing it with you, you can be sure she is doing it with someone else too.

Now, I know gold diggers may have a negative reputation, but hear me out. They can actually be pretty easy to deal with. They tend to be agreeable, they will listen to you, and they will do things for you that a regular woman would not even consider, as long as the money keeps flowing.

So my suggestion is this. If you cannot keep up financially, be honest. Yes, I said it. Be honest with a gold digger. Believe it or not, gold diggers often like the people they dig for gold from. They have feelings too. Just let them know that you may not have all the funds they desire.

Be straightforward. Say something like, "Hey, I am not exactly rolling in dough, but I can still make things happen." Gold diggers are usually meant for the rich and wealthy. Those men often do not have the time or patience for romance or for getting to know someone on a deeper level. For them, gold diggers fit the arrangement perfectly.

It becomes a transactional relationship. You pay, and they obey. Simple as that.

Now, how do you spot a gold digger? Well, it is not always easy, my friend. But here are a few questions you can ask.

First, ask them what they do for a living. If they say "nothing," that is a pretty big indicator, is it not? Gold diggers usually have no career aspirations or long-term dreams. Their primary goal is to find a wealthy man who will take care of them for life. You will not find many gold diggers with jobs, trust me. They do not have jobs. They are the job.

Another question to ask is where they see themselves in five years. A gold digger usually will not care much about that. They are living their best life right now because their main goal is simply finding a sugar daddy.

Here is a bonus tip. If they start showing a strong interest in your material possessions, such as your fancy car, big house, or high-paying job, then congratulations, my friend. You may have just hit the gold digger jackpot.

But be careful not to flaunt your wealth too much. Once they figure out how much you are worth, they may begin thinking about how to take it all from you.

Now, if you are not exactly wealthy or successful, do not worry. Gold diggers will not give you the time of day. You simply have nothing they are looking for. They are focused almost entirely on material things.

They may look stunning on the outside, but inside there is often very little substance. Conversations with a gold digger can feel quite shallow. They have rarely had to develop deep conversational skills because their beauty and charm have always done most of the work for them.

So do not expect discussions about philosophy, literature, or current events. They are usually more interested in the latest fashion trends, celebrity gossip, and luxurious vacations. Their world revolves around material possessions and the glamorous lifestyle that comes with them.

Now, I must emphasize that not all women who enjoy nice things or have high standards are gold diggers. It is important not to jump to conclusions or make assumptions about someone's intentions based solely on their preferences or lifestyle. The key is understanding the difference between someone who appreciates the finer things in life and someone who is only seeking financial gain in a relationship.

If you do find yourself attracted to a woman who seems to have a taste for luxury, take the time to get to know her beyond the surface level. Look for qualities such as genuine care, kindness, and compatibility. A true connection is built on more than material wealth alone.

Remember that a healthy and fulfilling relationship is based on mutual respect, trust, and emotional support, not on the size of your bank account.

In the end, it is up to you to decide what kind of relationship you want to pursue. If you are looking for a genuine and meaningful connection, focus on finding someone who values you for who you are as a person rather than for what you can provide financially.

Relationships built on shared interests, emotional connection, and personal growth are far more likely to withstand the test of time.

But if you choose to engage with a gold digger, proceed with caution. Be aware of the potential risks and understand the dynamics of that kind of relationship. Remember that it is essential to set boundaries and make sure your own needs and well-being are being met. And always keep in mind that true happiness and fulfillment come from genuine love and connection, not from the size of your bank account.

You see, gold diggers tend to focus on surface-level things. Many of them have never really needed to develop deep conversational skills because their beauty has often done the talking for them. People have always been willing to throw themselves, and their money, at these women. So do not expect deep intellectual discussions or profound insights from a gold digger. They are usually more interested in the latest fashion trends and celebrity gossip than anything else.

Now here is another thing about gold diggers. If you are a wealthy man with very little time to spare, they might actually suit your lifestyle. They are unlikely to question your actions or constantly demand your attention. As long as the money keeps flowing, they will often stay by your side without asking many questions.

In that type of arrangement, a man may feel free to have multiple women, lie, cheat, and live however he pleases because the relationship is based on money rather than emotional commitment. In the end, it becomes a purely transactional relationship.

But let me warn you, my friend. If you have financial goals and aspirations, if you are striving for success and hoping to build a meaningful future, stay far away from these women. Sure, you might eventually reach your goals, but a gold digger will drain your bank account along the way and leave you feeling foolish for ever believing their empty promises.

And let me tell you, these women have expensive taste. They want the finest things in life and will rarely settle for anything less. It is like dating a high-maintenance sports car. The moment you default on that car loan, it gets repossessed. And whenever it needs maintenance, you better be ready to pay up.

Trust me, gold diggers do not last long. Eventually they either crash and burn or move on to the highest bidder.

So my friend, be cautious when dealing with gold diggers. They may seem enticing at first because of their looks and charm, but remember that there is often very little substance beneath the surface.

If you are looking for a genuine connection and a partner who values you for who you are, steer clear of these materialistic temptations. Find someone who appreciates you for more than just your wallet.

After all, a good woman is like a reliable car that can go the distance, while a gold digger is like a flashy sports car that may look impressive at first but will eventually leave you bankrupt and broken-hearted.

But hey, I will not judge if you still want to dip your toes into the world of gold diggers. Just remember to protect your heart and your wallet along the way.

Good luck, my friend. May you find the love and happiness you truly deserve, whether it is with a gold digger or with someone who values you for all that you are.

# CHAPTER 23
## The Good Woman Archetype

A good woman is someone who allows you to grow and be your authentic self and, most importantly, loves you for who you are. Her primary concern is your happiness and well-being. This is often shown through acts of cooking and providing nourishment, as the saying goes, "The way to a man's heart is through his stomach." Unfortunately, in modern times, some women misunderstand this idea and believe that the way to a man's heart is through physical appearance alone.

A real woman understands that love involves supporting one another and helping each other achieve their goals. She is aware of the different archetypes of women and consciously chooses not to associate with them. If she does encounter such individuals, she may maintain a distant friendship or try to guide them toward maturity and a better understanding of what it means to be a responsible and mature woman.

A mature woman can be compared to a beautiful sunrise on a serene beach, while an immature woman is like a hurricane or tornado, causing destruction wherever she goes. This comparison highlights the importance of finding the right woman who brings positivity and stability into your life.

A good woman doesn't allow you to self-destruct or compromise your standards. She holds you accountable for your actions while still loving and supporting you. Love is grounded in truth, and a real woman will not lie to you. While she may occasionally tell small white lies to boost your confidence, she still values honesty and sincerity.

Good women are like family. They want to see you at your best and are willing to support you as you work toward your goals and fulfill your needs.

To keep a good woman, it is crucial to recognize and appreciate her value. Pay attention to her, communicate with her, and make effective communication a priority in your relationship. Communication is the key to maintaining a healthy and successful partnership.

Think of a good woman as a mirror. The way you treat her will often be reflected back to you. If you yell at her, she may yell back. If you ignore her, she may begin to ignore you. If you cheat on her, she may feel hurt and seek revenge.

Good women are often willing to follow your lead, but that also means they may reflect your behavior. If you display poor leadership or engage in negative actions, they may respond in similar ways. It is important for men to understand that sometimes we are the problem in relationships.

Women and men often see things differently, but communication helps bridge the gap between those differences. Without communication, growth becomes difficult and misunderstandings begin to take over.

A good woman is not easily influenced or manipulated by materialistic things. She understands the bigger picture of life and values the qualities that build character and substance. Some of the greatest joys and treasures in life cannot be touched or bought. They are emotional and meaningful things such as love, happiness, and togetherness.

If you find a woman who embodies these values, then you have found a good woman. Remember, love cannot be bought. It is given freely and genuinely.

Now, I know good women are hard to come by these days, but let me tell you what they are all about. A good woman is self-sufficient, yet she still allows a man to take the lead. It is not because she cannot handle things herself, but because she understands the natural balance of a relationship.

A good woman loves you for who you are, not for what you can buy or do for her. She sees beyond the material things and values the person behind them.

On the other hand, a succubus feeds off your material value. When you can no longer provide, she will drive you crazy and strip away your sense of manhood. And let me tell you, that is not a pretty sight.

It is time to break this cycle, my fellow men. Put your foot down and reclaim your identity. Real women are attracted to men who know who they are and what they want in life.

# CHAPTER 24

## Do Not Burn Bridges, You May Have To Cross Them One Day

D on't burn bridges," they say, cautioning us against severing ties that might one day prove essential. It is a lesson I learned the hard way, especially during my time in the music industry. I had aspirations of making it big and being recognized as one of the greatest producers in Atlanta, a title that some of my peers even bestowed upon me. But despite my talent, I found myself sidelined, not because of a lack of skill, but because of the bridges I carelessly burned along the way.

In the music business, as in life, relationships are everything. Some of the most talented artists I have met never made it big simply because they lacked the right connections. On the other hand, you will find some of the worst rappers and singers thriving, all because they cultivated relationships that kept them afloat. At times, the industry feels like a popularity contest, and that was a lesson I had to learn the hard way.

I have always had a bit of a temper. If I sensed injustice or felt wronged, I reacted explosively. Imagine Zeus hurling lightning bolts. My anger often came out in a similar fashion. I had a point to prove, and many times I was right. But being right doesn't always mean you should lash out. Sometimes diplomacy is far more powerful than righteousness.

The power of discernment becomes crucial in moments like these. You have to understand that everyone is fighting their own battles, just as you are. The world doesn't revolve around your perspective, and trying to control every situation will only lead to isolation. I burned bridges with people I could have collaborated with, people who might have helped elevate my career.

I often reflect on those moments. There were many times when I lashed out at someone, only to later find myself needing their support. People remember how you treat them, and those memories can linger like smoke from a burned bridge.

When you burn bridges, you limit your future options. You may find yourself forced to take a longer and more difficult route to achieve your goals. The music industry, like any other industry, is built on relationships. If you do not nurture them, you risk being blackballed. One influential person can spread the word that you are difficult to work with, and suddenly opportunities begin to disappear.

In my experience, I eventually learned to approach interactions with a mindset of learning and analysis. It is important to step back and reflect before responding. Quick reactions often lead to regret. The best move is not always to engage in conflict. Sometimes walking away with your integrity intact is the wisest choice.

I will admit that I am not exactly a people person. I have witnessed some of the worst behaviors in others, and it can be disheartening. However, the reality is that if you want to thrive in any field, you need people. You cannot make money or build a career in isolation. Your words and actions carry weight, and one careless misstep can cost you everything.

I once had a job that many people would consider a dream role. As a conductor for the railroad, I was respected, had a stable life, and a loving family. But one day I made choices that would alter the course of my life. Under the influence of drugs and alcohol, I fell asleep on the job. It was a dangerous mistake that could have had catastrophic consequences. In my reckless state, I lashed out at my coworkers, cursing and blaming them for my problems.

That day marked the beginning of a downward spiral. I lost my job, which eventually led to losing my family and falling into a cycle of anger and despair. I had been one of the best conductors, but my actions and my attitude burned that bridge forever. I became blackballed in the industry, and no matter how skilled I was, my behavior overshadowed my talent.

Looking back, I realize how selfish and reckless I was. I could have harmed someone, and the thought still terrifies me. I deserved the consequences I faced, and while I do not regret learning the lesson, I wish I had learned it in a different way. Sometimes hardship forces you to confront who you really are and recognize what needs to change.

The key lesson is to avoid dragging others into your turmoil. Your problems are ultimately your responsibility, and involving others in your anger can destroy relationships that might otherwise uplift you.

So as you navigate your own journey, remember this: do not burn bridges. Treat people with respect and kindness, even when tempers rise. You never know when you might need to cross that bridge again. By building and maintaining healthy relationships, you create a support system that can help carry you forward. Keep your bridges intact, and you may find that the road ahead becomes much easier to travel.

# CHAPTER 25

## Ignorance Is Bliss (Forrest Gump)

Let me tell you a story, one that is as rich and layered as a chocolate cake, with just enough comedic frosting to make it palatable. This tale revolves around a young man who, despite the odds stacked against him, managed to carve out a life that was anything but ordinary.

Picture this: a kid named Forrest who walked with braces on his legs, moving through life with a gait that was part shuffle and part shuffleboard. He was the target of countless bullies who seemed to derive endless joy from chasing him around and yelling insults that would make a sailor blush. But one fateful day, driven by the primal instinct of survival, Forrest sprinted like a gazelle, braces be damned.

This was no ordinary sprint. It was a revelation. In that moment, he transformed from the butt of every joke into a star in the making. His best friend Jenny was by his side, and together they navigated the turbulent waters of adolescence. She loved him fiercely, even while wrestling with her own complicated life choices that eventually led her to dance under neon lights.

Forrest, however, saw the world through a different lens, one that did not focus on societal norms or expectations. He loved Jenny for who she was, not for what she did. That is a testament to his heart, which was as big as Texas.

As Forrest grew older, the world remained unkind. He was still called "stupid," yet his speed caught the attention of the local football team. In an unexpected twist that would make even the most seasoned screenwriter giddy, he earned a scholarship to college and went on to win a national championship. Picture him in a football uniform, a far cry from the kid who once struggled just to walk.

But the twists did not end there. Forrest joined the military and, armed with his unyielding spirit, rescued an entire battalion, perhaps still searching for a little boy named Jimmy who had once shared the playground with him.

Yet it was Jenny who truly captured his heart, despite the struggles she faced. She was not the quintessential "good girl." She was a stripper who lived life on her own terms. Still, Forrest loved her without reservation, proving that love doesn't require society's approval. Life is messy, and sometimes the people we care about most do not fit neatly into the boxes the world tries to place them in.

Forrest's journey was filled with remarkable achievements. He became a ping-pong champion, sailed the high seas on a shrimp boat, and eventually amassed a fortune. But here is the kicker. He would often recount the story of his life to an elderly woman sitting beside him on a park bench while he waited for the bus.

The irony was not lost on him. He had lived a life full of adventure and triumph, yet at heart he remained a simple man who never worried too much about the small stuff.

So what is the point of this whimsical yet profound tale? The character of Forrest Gump embodies the essence of the phrase "ignorance is bliss." He faced adversity head-on, yet somehow remained untouched by the weight of the world's judgments. His lack of concern for societal expectations allowed him to move through life with a carefree spirit, like a kid running through a field of daisies. In this sense, ignorance became his superpower.

Consider the news, that constant barrage of negativity that fills our screens and minds with dread. Every time someone asks if

I have heard about the latest political scandal or natural disaster, I simply smile and shake my head. "Nope," I say, "and I am better off for it." Staying informed can sometimes feel like being trapped in a cage of anxiety, where every headline adds another weight to your shoulders. Why burden yourself with the chaos of the world when you can focus on the joy of your own life?

Imagine if, as children, we were told the exact time and place of our demise. We would not truly live. We would simply exist in a constant state of fear. Life is unpredictable, and that unpredictability is part of what makes it beautiful.

By not knowing everything, we are free to play our own game, unburdened by the score. Just like Forrest, who never obsessed over the scorecard of life. He simply kept running, kept living, and kept loving.

In this age of information overload, it is crucial to cultivate your mind like a garden. You can choose what to plant, whether it is flowers of positivity or weeds of negativity. The media can be a double-edged sword. It has the power to inform, but it can also distort reality. The choice of how you engage with it ultimately lies in your hands.

You do not have to watch reality shows that drain your spirit or news programs that fuel your anxiety. Instead, take control and curate your mental environment.

So take a page from Forrest's book. Embrace the beauty of not knowing everything. Focus on your own experiences, nurture your relationships, and allow the world to unfold as it will. Life is too short to be weighed down by endless "what ifs" and "should haves."

Choose joy. Choose love. Above all, choose to live your life with the heart of a child: carefree, curious, and blissfully ignorant. After all, ignorance, when used wisely, can indeed be a form of bliss.

# CHAPTER 26
## Failures Are More Valuable Than Success

In the grand tapestry of life, we all yearn for victory. Winning feels glorious, a sweet taste of accomplishment that can make even the most mundane moments sparkle. But let's face it. The path to success is often paved with failures, and without those bumps in the road, we would never appreciate our triumphs nearly as much.

Life is all about duality. Think about day and night. Without darkness, we would never truly cherish the light. In the same way, winning becomes meaningless if you have never tasted the bitter flavor of losing.

Failure is not just a setback. It is a teacher, a quirky mentor nudging you toward growth and understanding. When you stumble, you inevitably enter the pity party phase where disappointment seems to reign supreme. But do not be fooled. This is where the real magic happens.

Consider athletes. Yes, they may possess natural talent, but without the grind of consistent practice and the occasional loss, they would never achieve greatness. Success is a process, not just a destination. No one is born a master. We refine our skills over time, and every loss becomes another stepping stone toward that elusive win.

When you finally achieve victory, all those previous failures come together and take on new meaning. Your experiences become a treasure chest of lessons that make the victory feel even sweeter.

Think about it: most successful individuals have compelling backstories filled with obstacles such as poverty, adversity, or being underestimated. Contrast that with trust-fund kids, who often find themselves floundering, burdened by the weight of privilege without the grit that comes from struggle. Would you rather be handed everything at the start, only to feel empty at the finish, or face hardships early on and emerge triumphant and fulfilled?

This is the complexity of life, and embracing failure is crucial. Perspective is key; those who do not succeed often take losses personally and miss the valuable lessons embedded in each setback. Life is designed this way. We must embrace our failures in order to learn and evolve.

Self-reflection is vital: take responsibility for your stumbles, extract the wisdom hidden within them, and strive not to repeat the same mistakes. If you are stuck in a cycle of failure, that is not just bad luck; it is a habit.

The journey of growth is perpetual. Perfection is a myth, but the pursuit of learning is what makes life rich. Remember Bruce Lee's wisdom: some people simply do not know how to lose, and therein lies the crux of the issue.

To thrive, you must be fearless in the arena of success. If you fear losing, you will inevitably lose; but if you learn to embrace failure, you might just find the winning path waiting for you.

# CHAPTER 27

# The Law Of Accumulation (Money Laws)

L et's dive into the concept of **accumulation**, the gradual build-up of small actions that lead to significant outcomes. Whether it involves money, knowledge, or personal growth, accumulation is about saving and compounding those efforts over time. It is the little things done consistently that culminate in big successes.

**The 10% Rule**

When it comes to money, I am still learning, but one foundational lesson I have embraced is the **10% rule**. This principle, highlighted in the book *The Richest Man in Babylon*, suggests that you should save 10% of everything you earn and treat it like a treasure. This savings should not be spent frivolously. Instead, it should be invested to generate more wealth.

Think about it. If you set aside 10% of your paycheck each month, over three to four years you could accumulate thousands of dollars. And that money can work for you, generating even more wealth. Money is like a living entity. It can grow, multiply, and create a cycle of wealth. It is similar to a pyramid structure, but in a legal and ethical way. If you allow your money to make more money, you will eventually find yourself in a stronger financial position.

**The Boring Path to Wealth**

It is tempting to indulge in the excitement of spending, whether that means going out, hitting the club, or buying the latest gadgets. But the truth is that it is far more valuable to be boring and save your money. Excitement often comes with a hefty price tag, and those experiences might not add up to the value you think they do. Instead, focus on accumulating wealth.

Stay home and save your money. When you reach a certain financial milestone, then plan that vacation or special outing. Too often, people engage in activities that waste both money and time. Remember, time is money, and every dollar spent without purpose is essentially wasted.

You cannot get time back, but you can earn money again. However, reckless spending can lead to situations where recovering that money becomes increasingly difficult. The key is to prioritize saving and accumulating wealth before indulging in unnecessary expenses.

**The Reality of Debt**

Let's talk about debt for a moment. It is a burden that keeps many people trapped. When emergencies arise, such as a car transmission failing, individuals often find themselves without the funds to fix the problem, which leads to even more debt. They might end up purchasing another car, only to dig themselves deeper into financial trouble.

Debt can feel like modern-day slavery. If you are making payments on loans, credit cards, or services like Verizon or Netflix, you are essentially tied to those debts. The longer you wait to pay them off, the more you end up working for someone else rather than for yourself.

The path to financial freedom is to tackle your debt head-on. Start by allocating a portion of your income, for example 10%, to chip away at what you owe. As you work toward becoming debt-free, you will find that your financial situation improves significantly. Until you clear your debts, you do not truly have control over your finances.

**Personal Accumulation**

Accumulation is not just about money. It extends to all aspects of life, including health and personal development. For instance, I go to the gym six days a week. It may seem excessive, but I know that over time those small, consistent efforts will lead to significant gains in strength, endurance, and overall well-being.

Just like with finances, the discipline of consistent exercise and healthy eating accumulates into a strong mind and body. This discipline helps you make better decisions and can enhance your longevity in life.

**Value and Contribution**

Ultimately, accumulation shapes who we are. If you have nothing to offer, you become a burden rather than a contributor. It may sound harsh, but if you struggle financially, it is crucial to begin accumulating wealth as soon as possible. If you do not, you may eventually find yourself in dire straits, scrambling to figure out your next steps.

Self-discipline is vital. You must learn to say no to yourself, to others, and to distractions that pull you away from your goals. Doing what is difficult now will allow you to live more easily later.

In conclusion, start accumulating. Whether it is money, knowledge, or personal growth, every small effort counts. The journey to success is built on the foundation of consistent and disciplined actions that, over time, lead to extraordinary results. Set your sights on what you want to achieve and begin the process of accumulation today.

# CHAPTER 28
## The Law Of Moderation

Moderation is one of my favorite concepts, and I learned its value from a surprising source, my cousin. Growing up, I was always amazed by his seemingly endless supply of money. At one point, he had dabbled in selling drugs, but after learning his lessons, he transitioned into owning restaurants and clubs in Atlanta. These were not just ordinary establishments. They were popular venues that drew crowds and created buzz.

Curious about his wealth, I once asked him, "How do you have so much money?" His answer left me puzzled at first. "I live in moderation," he said. I did not quite understand what he meant, so I pressed him for more details. He explained that even though he had over $100,000 in the bank, he still drove an old, paid-off car. He did not indulge in excessive drinking or lavish spending. To me, it seemed strange. How could he afford so much yet choose a lifestyle that appeared so humble?

As I grew older and began to understand the essence of moderation, everything clicked into place. He was living proof that you can enjoy life without overindulgence. The key takeaway is that nothing is inherently bad. It is how we approach things that determines their impact on our lives.

**The Importance of Balance**

Take water, for example. It is essential for survival, yet too much of it can be deadly. The same principle applies to work. If you overwork yourself, you will eventually burn out. Enjoyment is important, but if you party too hard, you may find yourself broke or facing serious consequences. The trick is to approach every aspect of life with moderation.

Drinking is another example. It is perfectly fine to enjoy a drink occasionally, but going out every night to get drunk can lead to serious repercussions, including hospital visits, legal troubles, and financial strain. Learning to spend moderately helps you appreciate the value of a dollar and prevents wasteful habits.

Living modestly doesn't mean you are missing out. Rather, it allows you to keep your head down, stay focused, and carve your own path. What may look like moderation to you can appear as spectacular success to someone else. It is all about perspective and balance.

While I believe that a bit of obsession and craziness can drive you toward your goals, moderation is essential in everyday activities. Overindulgence in any area can lead to imbalances that affect other aspects of your life.

**The Consequences of Excess**

Moderation is crucial for personal growth. It can lead to a longer, healthier life and foster respect from others. When you approach things with moderation, you are more likely to achieve your dreams.

Consider driving. If you drive moderately, you are less likely to get a speeding ticket, waste fuel, or endanger yourself and others. In contrast, if you speed, you risk accidents, legal problems, and wasted resources. This analogy holds true across all areas of life. Overdoing anything can have life-altering consequences.

This is why the law of moderation is so powerful. In the grand scheme of things, moderation can be the difference between success and failure, health and illness, or even life and death. Embracing moderation allows you to enjoy life's pleasures without falling into the traps of excess.

As you navigate your journey, remember that moderation is key. It is not just about avoiding extremes; it is about finding a sustainable way to live and thrive. By embracing this principle, you can foster a balanced life that leads to personal fulfillment and long-term success.

# CHAPTER 29
## Do What Others Do Not

L ife is a journey that requires us to venture where others fear to tread. It demands dedication, sacrifice, and an unwavering commitment to self-improvement. While most people seek comfort and immediate gratification, those who truly aspire to greatness understand the importance of going against the grain.

While your friends are out partying, indulging in vices, and chasing temporary pleasures, you will be the one putting in the extra hours. You will be the one working tirelessly to build a future that will sustain not only yourself but also your loved ones. Most people dream of success, but they fail to realize that dreams alone will not make them a reality. Dreams, like seeds, must be nurtured, watered, and cared for. Only then can they grow into towering oak trees that rise above the rest.

You must live your life like a tree, steadfast and unyielding. A tree doesn't move unless it is dead, yet it constantly grows and adapts to adversity and failure. People may try to bring you down, but they forget that you are like a plant, destined to grow bigger and stronger through challenges. Those who never try will never fail, but they will also never truly succeed. The more you work and the more you try, the greater your chances of becoming a winner.

Life is a constant process of building. If you are not building, you are tearing down. Each step brings you closer to your goals, and even if you stumble and fall, you have learned how to climb. Those who choose not to walk this path may ridicule you, but remember that all great people face ridicule. They crucified Jesus, so what makes you immune? Let their words become mere noise, because at the end of the day they cannot undermine your ascent to the mountaintop.

Sometimes you will have to leave behind those who did not put in the work. They chose to remain stagnant while you strived for growth. In essence, they failed, and you cannot go back to rescue them. You have reached the pinnacle, and they must climb on their own. Life can be lonely and challenging at times, but it is during the hard moments that your true character shines. It is in the darkness that your light emerges.

Just like a caterpillar entering its cocoon, you too must go through a transformative process. Nurture your growth and nourish yourself physically, mentally, and spiritually. Strengthen your body, for it is the vessel that carries you through life. Cultivate your mind through meditation and mindfulness, allowing yourself to make logical decisions rather than succumbing to emotional impulses. In your spirit, find the resilience to keep pushing forward, even when the results have yet to appear.

To the aspiring athlete who dreams of going pro, while your teammates are out partying, be like Kobe Bryant and dedicate yourself to practice in the gym. To the artist yearning to become a genius, embrace your creativity and let your accomplishments inspire others. And to the man striving to provide for his family, remember that perseverance will eventually lead to prosperity.

If you dare to do what others will not, you will become what others only dream of becoming. The path less traveled may be challenging, but it is on this path that you will find true fulfillment and purpose. So, my dear reader, let us embark on this journey together, always striving to become the best versions of ourselves and embracing the endless possibilities that lie ahead.

**Continued: Step by Step to Greatness**

As we continue along the path less traveled, it is essential to delve deeper into the mindset and actions required to achieve greatness. This chapter explores the qualities and practices that separate those who settle for mediocrity from those who strive for excellence.

## 1.  Discipline

Success demands discipline. It requires waking up early, putting in extra effort, and consistently working toward your goals. While others may choose to indulge in distractions, you remain focused and committed to your journey. Discipline is the backbone of achievement and provides the structure necessary to overcome obstacles and stay on track.

## 2.  Perseverance

The road to success is paved with setbacks and failures. It is during these challenging times that your perseverance becomes essential. Embrace failure as a valuable lesson. Learn from it and use it as a stepping stone toward growth. Remember that every successful person has faced adversity, but it is their unwavering determination that sets them apart.

## 3.  Continuous Learning

Greatness is not achieved through complacency. It requires a thirst for knowledge and a commitment to continuous learning. Seek opportunities to expand your skills, broaden your horizons, and stay ahead of the curve. Embrace a growth mindset and remain open to new ideas and perspectives that can fuel your personal and professional development.

## 4.  Resilience

Life will test your resilience and present unexpected challenges. It is important to develop the ability to recover from setbacks and adapt to change. Maintain a positive mindset and view obstacles as opportunities for growth. Cultivate resilience by building a strong support network, practicing self-care, and nurturing your mental and emotional well-being.

## 5. Focus

In a world filled with distractions, maintaining focus is crucial. Define your priorities and align your actions with your goals. Avoid getting caught up in unnecessary noise and remain dedicated to your path. Develop strategies to minimize distractions, whether through setting boundaries, practicing mindfulness, or creating an environment that supports concentration.

## 6. Courage

To venture down the path less traveled requires courage. It means stepping outside your comfort zone and taking risks. Embrace the unknown, because it is where growth and discovery exist. Have courage in your convictions and the confidence to pursue your dreams, even when faced with uncertainty or criticism.

## 7. Persistence

Success rarely comes overnight. It requires persistence and a refusal to give up. Embrace a long-term perspective and understand that progress takes time. Stay committed to your vision, even when faced with setbacks or slow progress. The journey may be difficult, but the destination is worth the effort.

## 8. Self-Belief

Belief in yourself is a powerful force. Cultivate confidence and trust in your abilities. Surround yourself with a supportive community that uplifts and encourages you. Celebrate your successes, no matter how small, and use them as fuel to propel you forward.

As you continue on the path less traveled, embody these qualities and practices. Embrace the challenges, setbacks, and sacrifices, knowing that they are all part of the journey toward greatness. Stay true to yourself, remain dedicated, and never lose sight of the incredible potential that lies within you.

Remember, my dear reader, the path less traveled may be demanding, but it is on this path that you will discover your true strength and resilience, along with the extraordinary heights you are capable of reaching.

# CHAPTER 30

## Jealousy Is a Female Trait (Don't Be a Hater)

**Don't Be a Hater: Embracing Opportunities and Rising Above Envy**

In life, I've had my fair share of opportunities. I won't lie, I've been pretty lucky. But you know what they say: with great opportunities comes great envy and jealousy. It's like some haters can't handle the fact that I've got something they don't. And what exactly is that something? Well, it's not just about luck or natural talent. It's about the resources and advantages that I've been blessed with.

Let me take you back to my childhood in College Park, Georgia. If you know anything about Atlanta, you know that College Park isn't exactly the lap of luxury. It's not the kind of place where you'll find gold-plated sidewalks or diamond-studded street signs. It's more like the hood, if you catch my drift. But here's the thing: College Park has a rich history. It used to be predominantly white until middle-class African American families moved in. When they arrived, many white residents packed their bags and headed north, leaving the neighborhood to African American families. Over time, the cost of living rose, and some of those middle-class families found themselves struggling to make ends meet. But my family managed to remain middle class and upstanding.

Growing up, I had a lot of friends. They would come over to my house, and boy, did they have a lot to say. They would marvel at my "huge" house and comment on how clean it was. They thought I had everything they could only dream of. But here's the kicker: my house was just as big as theirs. The difference was that I had a more structured family life and better living conditions. My parents paid their taxes, provided us with a roof over our heads, and made sure we had the things we needed. They instilled in us the importance of education and of being responsible members of society. So yeah, my house may have seemed like a mansion to my friends, but it was really just the result of a little thing called discipline.

And let's not forget the whole "not black enough" ordeal. Oh boy, did I get teased for that. Apparently, because I didn't speak the same way as my friends, I wasn't "black" enough for them. It's funny how language and culture can create such divides, isn't it? But here's the truth: I grew up around different kinds of people, and my parents raised me to be adaptable in any situation. So yeah, I may not have used the same vernacular as my friends, but that didn't make me any less black. It just made me versatile.

As I got older, I started realizing that having more than others made some people envious. It's like they couldn't handle the fact that I was doing better than they were. In college, I made the mistake of letting my friends crash at my place. Let's just say it didn't end well. They turned my house into a never-ending party, neglected basic cleanliness, and even brought illegal substances into my home. Talk about taking advantage of my generosity. That experience taught me a valuable lesson about the toxic effects of envy and how it can make people forget about boundaries and respect.

But you know what? Despite the haters, I managed to graduate from college and become a board-certified behavior analyst. Meanwhile, some of those same friends are still stuck working in factories, riding forklifts all day long. I guess they never quite figured out how to channel their envy into motivation. Too bad for them.

Now, don't get me wrong. I'm not immune to jealousy. I've had my fair share of moments when I wished I had what someone else had. But instead of tearing them down or making them feel inferior, I learned to use their success as inspiration. After all, if they can do it, why can't I? Jealousy became a driving force that pushed me to strive harder and prove that I was doing something right.

It's funny how winners often attract hate and criticism. Just look at the New England Patriots and Tom Brady. They've won multiple Super Bowls, yet so many people despise them. Why? Because winners evoke envy and jealousy in those who can't achieve the same level of success. But here's the thing: being a hater or being jealous is counterproductive. Instead of tearing others down, it's better to congratulate them and use their success as inspiration to grow and move forward.

One thing I've learned on this journey is the importance of surrounding yourself with a supportive circle of friends. These are the people who uplift and encourage you, especially during moments of self-doubt. It's crucial to have friends who share your drive for success, because trust me, they'll help keep you on the right path. On the other hand, being around people who constantly hate on you and feel envious of your achievements is a recipe for disaster. These individuals want to keep you at their level, dragging you down with their negativity and preventing you from reaching your full potential.

It's important to strive for your best in all aspects of life. Cultivating discipline and consistency will lead to greatness in whatever you pursue. People who hate, gossip, and harbor jealousy usually lack these qualities. They remain stagnant and are unwilling to grow or learn from their mistakes. It's not your fault that they choose to stay at the bottom of the mountain while you strive for the top.

As you climb the ladder of success, you'll naturally encounter more haters and jealous individuals. But remember, their negativity is not a reflection of your worth or abilities. In fact, it's a testament to your progress. The more you accomplish, the more they'll try to tear you down. But don't give them the satisfaction. Don't fuel their fire with your energy and attention. Instead, focus on your own journey and surround yourself with genuine supporters who truly love you and want the best for you.

Being at the top of the mountain can be lonely, but it's a place where winners reside. Those who fit in and settle for mediocrity will always have a crowd of friends, but they'll never truly stand out. So why fit in when you can stand out? Embrace your uniqueness, your drive, and your ambition. Let the haters hate, but don't let their words or actions consume you.

Sometimes, the best way to defeat someone is simply by doing nothing at all. When you refuse to give energy to their hate, it eventually fizzles out. As you continue on your journey toward success, you'll encounter more people who envy and resent you. But remember, their feelings are their burden to bear, not yours. Stay focused, keep pushing forward, and let your achievements speak for themselves.

In the end, it's all about finding genuine love and support within your circle. Surround yourself with people who uplift you, encourage you, and celebrate your successes. These are the individuals who will motivate you to keep going, even when haters try to bring you down.

So don't be a hater. Embrace the opportunities that come your way and rise above the envy and jealousy that others may harbor. Your journey to success is yours alone, and it's up to you to make the most of it. Let the haters hate while you keep shining and reaching for the stars.

# CHAPTER 31

## You Are What You Eat! (Consumerism And Substance Abuse)

Have you ever heard the saying, "You are what you eat"? Well, it turns out that statement is actually true. But it's not just about food. It's about everything you put into your body. In this chapter, we'll explore how substances, both good and bad, can influence your mind, body, and soul.

Now, when we talk about substances, we're not just referring to drugs and alcohol. It goes beyond that. Substances can include anything from poor eating habits to not drinking enough water, or even the products you put on your skin. It can even extend to what you watch or consume on the internet. Anything that you consistently put into your body has an impact on your future.

Let me share my own story as an example. For about 20 years, I was a heavy drinker and drug user. It started off innocently enough, with a little bit of weed and some casual drinking. But over time, it escalated to prescription pills and other illegal substances. These choices had a negative impact on my life. My dreams and aspirations were shattered by my self-destructive behavior.

Drinking too much impaired my ability to communicate effectively and often led to embarrassing situations and ruined relationships. Smoking too much marijuana made me complacent and stagnant, preventing me from taking the necessary actions to achieve my goals. Substance abuse became a contributing factor in my divorce, job losses, and the pain I caused the people I loved.

Not to mention my constant legal issues, time spent in jail, and the financial burdens from DUIs, public intoxication charges, and disorderly conduct.

I'm so grateful for the knowledge and skills I have as a therapist, because they've played a crucial role in my personal journey toward healing and self-improvement. It wasn't an easy road, but I knew I had to make changes in order to turn my life around.

I found myself in a situation where I had to quit drinking and smoking, not because I wanted to, but because it was a condition set by the court. If I didn't comply, I would have faced further legal consequences. This forced me to confront my addictions head-on and make a conscious decision to let go of harmful substances.

In my pursuit of inner peace and well-being, I turned to deep breathing exercises, yoga, and meditation to calm my mind and nourish my soul. These practices helped me find a sense of inner balance and tranquility that I'd been missing for so long. Additionally, I incorporated regular exercise into my routine, aiming to detoxify my body and improve my overall health and fitness.

To rebuild my life, I embarked on new ventures and set new goals for myself. This not only stimulated my brain function but also instilled a sense of self-reliance and purpose. It was a gradual process that required patience and perseverance. Just as it took me two decades to become addicted, it took me nearly ten years to learn how to truly live my life again.

Breaking free from long-standing habits and addictions is a challenging journey, but it's possible with determination and the right support. Through therapy and self-care, I was able to rebuild my life and create a better future for my daughter, my family, and myself. It's a testament to the power of personal growth and the resilience of the human spirit.

But here's the thing: my story isn't unique. We all have our "aha" moments, our lowest points when we realize we need to change. And that's the key. Recognizing that when we're at our worst, we have the opportunity to get better and fix things.

Substances offer temporary happiness, but they come at the cost of long-term consequences. That momentary satisfaction may feel good in the present, but it ultimately holds us back from achieving greater things. It's a trade-off and a sacrifice we make.

Now, I'm not saying that all drinking and drug use is bad. After all, we have an entire medical system that relies on drugs to help people. But even too much of a good thing can be detrimental. Just like drinking too much water can be dangerous, overindulging in any activity or substance can have negative effects on your health.

Consider a person who constantly indulges in unhealthy eating habits. They may become overweight, which can affect their mental health and lead to sadness or depression. This can make them feel unmotivated and unable to take the necessary actions to improve their situation. What you put into your body directly impacts your mental health and overall well-being.

The same applies to those addicted to sex. Excessive sexual activity can lead to sexually transmitted diseases, unwanted pregnancies, and emotional baggage from past relationships. Even something as seemingly innocent as wearing too much makeup can have an impact on your skin and overall health, which can also affect your mindset.

Excessive exposure to negative programming can have a profound impact on our brains, often causing us to mirror what we see on TV or the Internet. It is crucial that we use these media platforms to enhance our lives rather than allowing them to disrupt our well-being. Just like using a hammer to drive a nail into a wall, we must use technology wisely. Misuse can lead to unintended consequences and the need for repairs.

Currently, social media, the Internet, and many TV outlets are often misused, resulting in negative social influences. They frequently present ideas that we may begin to adopt as our own, even when they do not align with our true selves. This is why it is essential to be mindful of what we consume. Sometimes what our eyes see can deceive us and distort our perception of reality.

By being conscious of the content we consume and the messages we internalize, we can protect ourselves from the negative effects of media and make informed choices about what aligns with our values and personal growth. Let us remember that we have the power to use technology as a tool for improvement and not allow it to control us.

The bottom line is that taking care of yourself is crucial. If you neglect your body, you neglect your mind and soul. Think of it like maintaining a brand-new car. If you don't keep it clean and perform regular maintenance, it will eventually break down. The same goes for your brain and body. Taking care of your health and being mindful of what you put into your body directly affects how well your brain functions.

Substances are everywhere. You can find them in the form of prescription drugs or on the streets. They can contribute to mental illnesses such as depression, schizophrenia, bipolar disorder, and other serious conditions. But here's the thing: substances themselves are not natural or God-given solutions. What is God-given is your ability to make choices. When you choose to pollute your body, you're essentially harming your mind and spirit.

Take cigarette smoking, for example. People who smoke for over 20 years are at a high risk of developing cancer. Do you know what's in a cigarette? Poison. Yet people continue to poison themselves. Why? Because deep down they may be struggling with depression or unresolved emotions and do not know how to face those feelings. The remedy is to detox and confront those uncomfortable emotions head-on, without relying on substances as a crutch.

Now you may have heard of support groups like Alcoholics Anonymous (AA). While these groups aim to help people struggling with substance abuse, they sometimes fall short. Why? Because they often focus heavily on reliving past episodes and blaming oneself for past mistakes. As a result, some individuals may not fully learn how to deal with everyday life challenges moving forward.

The key is to understand that the past is a learning lesson. We all make mistakes, but it's how we learn from them that truly matters. Instead of dwelling on the past, we should live in the present and embrace the future. Too many people get stuck living in the past, regretting the present, and fearing the future. Substances often play a significant role in perpetuating this cycle.

So what can you do to improve your well-being?

If you want to improve your well-being, there are several steps you can take. Let's take a closer look at some of these strategies.

**1.   Take care of your physical health:**

This includes maintaining a balanced diet, staying hydrated, and getting regular exercise. Eating nutritious foods and drinking enough water provide the essential nutrients your body needs to function properly. Exercise not only keeps you physically fit but also releases endorphins that boost your mood and overall well-being.

**2.   Prioritize sleep and stress management:**

Getting enough quality sleep is crucial for your mental and physical health. Sleep deprivation can lead to increased stress, impaired cognitive function, and a weakened immune system. Develop healthy sleep habits and incorporate stress management techniques such as meditation, deep breathing exercises, or activities that help you relax and unwind.

### 3. Seek professional help:

Therapy can be a valuable tool for addressing underlying issues and learning effective coping mechanisms. A therapist can guide you in developing healthy ways to deal with anxiety, stress, and other challenges in your life. They can provide support, guidance, and tools to help you navigate difficult times.

### 4. Surround yourself with a positive support system:

The people you surround yourself with have a significant impact on your well-being. Seek out friends and loved ones who uplift and inspire you. Build a supportive network of people who encourage your growth and share similar values. Surrounding yourself with positive influences can enhance your overall happiness and success.

### 5. Limit exposure to negative substances:

Be mindful of the substances you consume, both physically and mentally. Be conscious of what you watch, read, and listen to. Avoid excessive exposure to negative media, gossip, or toxic relationships. Instead, focus on consuming content that uplifts, educates, and inspires you.

### 6. Find healthy outlets for stress and emotions:

Instead of turning to substances as a coping mechanism, explore healthier alternatives. Engage in activities that bring you joy, such as hobbies, creative outlets, or spending time in nature. Find healthy ways to express your emotions, such as journaling, talking to a trusted friend, or practicing mindfulness.

### 7. Practice self-care:

Make self-care a priority in your life. This includes taking time for yourself, engaging in activities that bring you joy and relaxation, and prioritizing your physical and mental well-being. Self-care isn't selfish. It's necessary for maintaining a healthy balance in your life.

Remember, it's important to be patient with yourself and allow room for growth and self-improvement. Changing habits and patterns takes time and effort. By making conscious choices to prioritize your well-being and reduce the influence of negative substances, you can create a more fulfilling and joyful life.

# CHAPTER 32

## The Law Of Environments (You Are The Sum Of The 5 People You Are Closest Too)

Ever wondered why fish don't grow in a fishbowl? It's not because they lack potential. It's because they're limited by their environment. Just like a shark in a tiny tank, they can't grow beyond the confines of their surroundings. This concept applies to all aspects of life. If you find yourself struggling, it might be time to change the people around you. In fact, change your people, places, and things. Change your nouns, and you can change your life.

### The Influence of Your Circle

You are the sum of the five people you spend the most time with. If you're hanging around four losers, guess what? You'll likely be the fifth. Conversely, if you surround yourself with four winners, you'll eventually find success yourself. This isn't just motivational fluff. It's a fundamental truth. People grow according to their environment, and that includes the people within it.

Let's break it down. Can a tree thrive in a desert? Nope. Can a cactus survive in a rainforest? Not a chance. Can a bear live comfortably in a city? Definitely not. So why are you trying to grow in a limited environment with limited friends?

### The Right Surroundings Matter

If you aspire to excel in a particular profession, you need to immerse yourself in the right environment. Take music, for example. If you live in Montana and dream of becoming a musician, you might find it challenging to make it big. The music scene is sparse. Instead, you might be better off in Atlanta, where the beats and rhythms are alive.

Let's say you want to be a stockbroker. Living in Kansas might not be the best choice if you want to connect with the right people. Yes, technology expands possibilities, but being around like-minded individuals fosters growth and opportunity. It's simply illogical to remain a big fish in a small pond.

## The Football Player's Journey

I once knew a football player who was the star of his small-town team. Everyone adored him, and he earned a scholarship to play in college. But when he made it to the NFL, he quickly realized he was out of his league. Surrounded by exceptional talent, he lost his confidence. The praise he received back home didn't translate to the big stage, and eventually he quit. If he had trained with elite athletes earlier, perhaps he would have thrived instead of fading into obscurity.

This story illustrates a crucial point: who you hang around matters. Your circle of influence can either elevate you or drag you down.

## The Struggles of Social Acceptance

I've made the mistake of surrounding myself with the wrong crowd. I was drawn to the "in" crowd, the bad kids. Despite knowing right from wrong, I still wanted to fit in. This choice didn't just damage my potential. It also taught me a valuable lesson: sometimes it's better to walk alone than to compromise your values for acceptance.

Being alone can be a superpower. It allows you to focus on your thoughts, which are often more truthful than the opinions of others. Embracing solitude can lead to profound personal growth. You become less influenced by external pressures and more capable of following your own path.

**Learning Through Experience**

Let's face it: I can preach to you all day, but real growth comes from experience. You'll discover that some people who claim to care don't truly have your back. That girlfriend you thought was loyal might not be. That boyfriend who seems charming could turn out to be a slacker. Life is tough, but you must persevere because no one else will save you.

Just like plants and animals thrive in suitable habitats, you must seek the right environment to flourish. The most vibrant life forms exist where they can thrive, and the same applies to you. A palm tree won't grow in a snowy climate because it's a tropical plant.

**Choosing the Right Friends**

Don't tether yourself to mediocrity out of a desire for companionship. True friends are those who push you to be better. We often mistake acquaintances for friends, but as we grow older our circles become smaller. In elementary school, everyone is your friend. By high school, that number dwindles. In college, it shrinks even further. As you age, you might find that you can count your real friends on one hand.

Those who walk alongside you on your journey will help you up when you stumble. They'll encourage you to keep moving forward, and that's the essence of genuine friendship.

**Embrace Your Environment**

So as you navigate through life, remember the law of environments. Surround yourself with people who inspire growth, challenge you, and motivate you to reach new heights. Be aware of the influence your surroundings have on your potential. Embrace the power of your environment and watch as you evolve into the person you're meant to be.

In the end, the choice is yours. Will you remain in your fishbowl, or will you dare to swim in the vast ocean?

# CHAPTER 33
## The Purpose Of Man

In the realm of men and their pursuits, there exists a powerful stimulus that can often lead them astray from their true purpose in life: the insatiable desire for intimacy. Now, don't get me wrong, dear reader. There's nothing wrong with enjoying the company of women. However, when this desire takes precedence over your own journey, it's time to reevaluate your priorities.

As a man, your primary goal should be to fulfill your mission in life. Your mission is your purpose, the very reason you exist. Without a purpose, life becomes as meaningless as a one-legged man in a butt-kicking contest. And let's face it, our purpose is not solely to frolic around collecting phone numbers and engaging in amorous adventures. No, our purpose is to contribute value to this world using the unique gifts bestowed upon us by the divine.

So when you encounter a woman, it's crucial that you're at a stage in your life where you're actively pursuing your goals and are on a mission to achieve greatness. A truly captivating man is one who doesn't incessantly text or call a woman, because he understands that women are often drawn to those who exude an air of mystery. It's almost like fishing, my friend. You don't swim into the lake to catch a fish. You patiently wait and allow the fish to come to you. Similarly, a high-value man attracts beauty because he embodies confidence and purpose within himself.

Now let's address a pressing issue in today's world. Many men find themselves complaining about how women have taken on the role of men. But here's the truth. Women are only wearing the pants because many men have forgotten the true essence of manhood. As men, our duty is to protect, provide, and support. But how can we fulfill these responsibilities if we cannot even provide for ourselves?

I implore you, dear reader, to heed this advice: don't date women until you have your own place, pay your own bills, and achieve financial independence. How can you expect to sustain a woman if you cannot sustain yourself? Women, just like anyone else, desire security and protection. However, this is not their sole objective. Remember, we are all individuals with our own thoughts and desires.

There's a saying that some women are like putting your money in the bank, because they will show interest. But fear not, for there's a way to navigate these treacherous waters. Focus on fulfilling your purpose in life. Your purpose should be your guiding light, propelling you forward with purposeful strides. Without a purpose, you're simply spinning your wheels on an exercise bike, expending energy but going nowhere.

Take a year, my friend, just for yourself. Be selfish and invest in your own growth, health, and well-being. Strengthen your finances and ensure the security of your loved ones. Discover who you are and what truly motivates you. Only after this journey of self-discovery should you begin to consider inviting a woman into your life. But remember, don't give too much attention. A man who constantly showers a woman with compliments and treats her like a Greek goddess may lose sight of his own purpose and ambition.

Women, often without realizing it, are drawn to men who maintain focus on their own lives rather than constantly seeking attention from them. Attention can become a form of currency, and when it is given too freely it loses value. They may claim to want someone who worships the ground they walk on, but deep down many crave the challenge of earning genuine respect. When a woman spends time with you, think of it as her earning your valuable time, because your time could also be spent on other meaningful pursuits.

When you're in the company of a woman, be direct and intentional in your communication. Don't beat around the bush or waste her time. Learn to ask for what you want respectfully, and if she can't provide it, bid her farewell. There's no point investing your time, energy, and finances in someone who doesn't share your values or desires.

Remember, my fellow men, this world is filled with millions of beautiful women. Just because one doesn't align with your values doesn't mean another won't. Don't be afraid to walk away from those who don't contribute positively to your life. It takes wisdom and self-assurance to know what you truly want—and the discipline to avoid wasting time on negative influences.

Being a man isn't easy, and it becomes even more difficult when you're entangled with a woman who doesn't value or respect you. That's why it's important not to overwhelm a woman with constant validation. The more validation you give freely, the less attractive you become in her eyes. Validation should be earned through her actions, and if she falls short of that standard, she shouldn't receive the reward.

Let's shift the narrative, my friends. Men are the true prize in the game of life. There may be an abundance of women in this world, but there are far fewer men who possess the discipline, strength, and character that make them truly valuable. Men are the primary providers of the resources that help sustain and build the world around us. And while it's true that women can now earn their own money and support themselves, that reality doesn't erase the deeper dynamics rooted in our primal nature.

As men, we're wired to be the hunters, the providers, and the protectors. It's our duty to go out into the world and secure the resources necessary for survival, while women, in turn, take on the role of nurturing and caring for children. But when that balance shifts and a woman begins to provide more, it often leads to a loss of respect. Respect, my friend, is the invisible currency men thrive on. Without it, the fabric of human relationships begins to unravel.

To gain respect from others, you must first have self-respect. Your purpose and the goals that drive you give direction to your life and keep you focused on what truly matters. If a woman doesn't contribute to your bigger picture, then she's ultimately subtracting from your life. And trust me, my friend, when a woman subtracts, the dividends often end up going to her.

That's why it's crucial not to give a woman too much validation. When you shower her with constant attention and validation, she eventually grows bored and begins seeking validation elsewhere. A woman needs to feel like she's earned your validation, just as you've earned hers. It's a delicate dance, my friend, but when it's done with patience and finesse, it can bring immense satisfaction and fulfillment.

Being a man is no easy task, and it's even harder when you're entangled with a woman who doesn't value you for who you truly are. That's why it's important to align yourself with people who share your values and aspirations. This world is vast and filled with countless beautiful women. Don't be afraid to let go of those who don't align with your vision of a fulfilling life. Just as a wise fisherman knows when to release a fish back into the sea, you must have the wisdom to let go of those who don't contribute positively to your journey.

Remember, my friend, your purpose in life is of utmost importance. It is the guiding force that leads you toward greatness. Prioritize your purpose over the pursuit of women, and you'll find that the right woman, one who truly complements your life, will naturally gravitate toward you.

So, my dear reader, embrace your purpose, nurture your self-respect, and move through the world with the wisdom of a true man. And always remember, you are the prize in this grand adventure called life.

# CHAPTER 34
## The Cow And The Buffalo

The cow and the buffalo are fascinating creatures that share many similarities and belong to the same family. However, there are several key differences between them beyond their physical appearance. Did you know that cows and buffaloes possess a unique ability to sense when a storm is approaching? It's remarkable how nature has equipped them with this instinct.

When a storm is on the horizon, the cow instinctively runs away, seeking shelter before it arrives. At first glance, this may seem like a wise decision, but in reality it can be more harmful than helpful. While the cow flees from the storm, it fails to realize that the storm continues moving in the same direction. Eventually it catches up. As a result, the cow may spend days or even weeks enduring the harsh conditions of the storm while battling the cold and rain.

The buffalo, on the other hand, takes a completely different approach. When it senses a storm approaching, it runs directly toward it and confronts the toughest part, the heart of the storm. Surprisingly, as the storm passes over the buffalo, it quickly moves on, leaving the buffalo free to roam once again. In many ways the storm revitalizes the earth, nourishing the land and providing the buffalo with greener pastures.

Now let's reflect on this tale and ask ourselves an important question. Are we more like the cow or the buffalo when faced with challenges? Do we shy away from our problems, allowing them to persist until they eventually catch up with us? Or do we have the courage to confront our issues head on, knowing that by doing so we can overcome them?

Avoiding our problems may offer temporary relief, but those problems will continue to follow us until we gather the strength to face them. It takes immense bravery to confront our fears and face the storms of life. Only by doing so can we truly overcome adversity and emerge stronger on the other side.

Fear often paralyzes us and prevents us from taking action or seizing opportunities. However, it's important to remember that fear is often based on false evidence appearing real. We cannot predict the future, and dwelling on what might happen only slows our progress. Instead, we must focus on controlling our actions and embracing the storms that come our way.

As the comedian Jim Carrey once said, hope is walking through the fire, and faith is leaping over it. We must believe that whatever lies ahead isn't stronger than us. Like the buffalo, we may endure powerful storms, but it's important to remember that we have the strength to weather them. Why choose to live our lives like the cow, constantly running and dreading the rain?

By facing our fears and pushing through adversity, we build faith and confidence in ourselves. We learn valuable lessons, grow as individuals, and live with fewer regrets. Regret may feel safe in the moment, but over time it hardens the soul and fills the mind with endless thoughts of "what if." When we confront the storms of life head on, we free ourselves from that burden. We become stronger and happier, knowing we had the courage to face our fears and move forward, whether we succeeded or simply learned and grew.

So, my friend, let us choose to be like the buffalo. Let us walk through life with the courage to face challenges head on and embrace the storms that come our way. It is through these experiences that we discover true fulfillment and a lasting sense of purpose. Remember, the grass is greener on the other side of fear.

# CHAPTER 35
## Get Paid First

This chapter is short and straight to the point: **get paid first.** It's a lesson I had to learn the hard way, and I wish someone had drilled it into my head long before I had to experience it myself.

Never give away your ideas or services without securing some form of payment first. Payment doesn't always have to be cash. It can be any benefit or form of value that acknowledges your work. If you're giving away what you have without receiving anything in return, what's the point?

Don't talk yourself out of money. If you set a price, stick to it. Don't negotiate yourself down just to make someone else comfortable. Know your worth and stand by it. I've seen too many people talk themselves out of a fair price, offering discounts that devalue their skills and hard work. Why should someone get a discount? The value you provide is what it is. There shouldn't be a clearance sale on your expertise.

In the music industry, I learned this lesson the hard way. I sold my beats and production services, and I always made sure I was paid upfront before doing any work. Many people will tell you that you must collaborate for free to build your reputation and expand your network. I strongly disagree. Those who follow that advice often lose their creativity and intellectual property before they even get their foot in the door.

I've witnessed countless artists collaborate with others only to get taken advantage of. They complain that someone "robbed" them, but in reality they robbed themselves by failing to establish clear boundaries. They were eager to build relationships and be friendly, but that eagerness can easily lead to exploitation.

Business and friendship exist in two different realms. If you're providing a service or product, it must involve an exchange of equal value. That's the foundation of trade and money.

You must make sure you receive what your work is worth. You wouldn't walk into a store, pick up a product, and expect it for free just because you like the cashier, would you? The same principle applies to your work and creativity.

So remember, whether you're in music, art, or any other field, **get paid first.** Protect your worth and don't let anyone diminish the value of what you bring to the table. Your skills and ideas are valuable. Treat them accordingly.

# CHAPTER 36
## The Law Of Spell Casting

**The Power of Words and Beliefs**

In the early years of our education, we're taught numbers, shapes, and colors. Yet among all these lessons, one stands above the rest: learning how to spell and understand letters. This seemingly simple skill holds a profound power that many people either fail to recognize or refuse to believe in. It is the power of words, or what some might call the power of spells.

The power of the tongue is an extraordinary force. What we speak into the world carries energy and vibration that resonates throughout the universe, shaping our reality in one way or another. As children, learning to spell and communicate our thoughts and feelings gives us the ability to express ourselves clearly and effectively. Without this skill, our influence on others and our ability to achieve our goals diminishes greatly.

In the grand scheme of things, the universe is built upon two fundamental communication tools: numbers and letters. Numbers may hold great significance, but it is through letters that we interpret, explain, and give meaning to them. Communication is the foundation of every relationship and every endeavor in life. The better we communicate our thoughts and emotions, the more likely we are to achieve our goals and maintain strong connections with others.

But let's go deeper into the concept of spells. Back in the 15th century, witches were persecuted and condemned for practicing witchcraft. What many people failed to realize, however, was that every human being casts spells in their own way. The very people who condemned and executed these witches were casting spells themselves. The words they spoke reflected their beliefs and emotions toward these women, eventually leading to their condemnation and the erasure of their culture. In the end, it was all a matter of perception. When enough people believe in something, it becomes a shared reality.

Yet in truth, much of life is shaped by perception. It depends on how we choose to interpret what we see and experience. Take the color blue, for example. We call it blue, but what if it had been named purple instead? In reality, it is simply a label we assign in order to understand the world around us. Language helps us organize reality, but it also shapes how we experience it.

When we speak negatively about someone, we project our perception of that person. Those words not only affect them, but they also influence our own state of mind. Have you ever found yourself disliking someone and speaking negatively about them, only to discover that your words eventually reached their ears? This is rarely a coincidence. What we put into the world through our words often finds its way back to us. It becomes a reflection of the energy we carry. In many ways, it is like looking into a mirror.

On the other hand, have you ever wished someone well and spoken positively about their success? More often than not, those positive intentions return in unexpected ways. Sometimes we even realize that our words encouraged that person to move closer to their goals. This is why gossip ultimately harms the person who spreads it. The negative words we speak reinforce our own bitterness, and if the person we speak about hears them, the damage spreads further. Everything becomes clouded with negativity. For this reason, it is important to remain mindful of the words we choose and not allow negative influences to shape our beliefs.

Breaking free from the spell requires us to examine our beliefs and recognize that we have control over what we choose to believe. When people hurt us with their words, it often reflects how deeply we have internalized their judgment. We may begin to feel inadequate or incapable because of the beliefs imposed upon us by society. But when we remove those external beliefs and focus on what we truly believe about ourselves, the influence of the material world begins to lose its power over us.

Life is structured around systems of order. We label things, establish rules, and create laws. But who determines whether those laws are truly correct? Who decided that society should operate according to these principles? In the end, what matters most is what you believe about yourself and how you project your vision of life. Surrounding yourself with people who bring joy into your life and sincerely wish you well is essential. There will always be individuals who try to hold you back because they fear your growth or your success. They cast spells of negativity, telling you that you will never achieve your dreams or that certain paths are not meant for you. But who are they to judge what you should do when deep down you already know the direction you must take?

These proverbial crabs in a bucket ultimately hinder your growth and prevent you from reaching your full potential. The curse of one's environment is that we often become products of it. Even the most capable person cannot completely escape the influence of their surroundings. When you surround yourself with negative people who constantly speak ill of you and wish you no success, their spells begin to take effect. The crucial thing to remember about spells is that they only work if you believe in them.

For instance, there is an old folk tale that suggests placing salt in front of a door can prevent negative spirits from entering. While this may appear to be a simple superstition, it carries a deeper meaning. When someone sees salt placed in front of a door, they may pause and question why it is there. That hesitation often comes from a belief that something is wrong or out of place. On the other hand, a person with a pure spirit may walk through the door without fear and simply ask about its purpose, because they trust your intentions.

Another example is the practice of burning sage in a home. Some people believe it helps cleanse a space of negativity and invite positive energy. Yet it is not only about the physical act of burning sage. The true power lies in the intention behind the act and in how it is perceived. When you genuinely believe in its purpose and project that belief, others are more likely to respect it as well. So when someone who means you well enters your home and sees the sage burning, they may choose to leave out of respect for your desire to keep negativity away.

The words we speak hold immense power. They reflect our inner reality and reveal our emotional intelligence and patterns of thought. This is why it is important to pay attention to the words we choose. Our words should be clear, thoughtful, and aligned with our beliefs rather than driven by fleeting emotions. Emotions will always influence how we communicate, but true emotional intelligence comes from learning how to guide those emotions rather than projecting the wrong feelings onto others.

We all have disagreements and thoughts we keep to ourselves because that is simply part of life. No one is completely pure-hearted all the time. Therefore, we must learn to compartmentalize our emotions and express them in ways that do not cast negative spells on those around us. This is why certain words are considered curses and why we have what are known as curse words. When we speak negatively or cast harmful words toward someone, those words become a curse. And if the other person believes in them, they can begin to manifest in that person's reality.

These beliefs and spells have deep roots in the past. Throughout history, people who presented alternative schools of thought or challenged established social structures were often persecuted and condemned. Those who thought differently were seen as threats because they challenged the norms of society. If enslaved people had been allowed to read and gain knowledge, they would have been more capable of rising against their oppressors. Systems of power rarely encourage that kind of awakening. Instead, they encourage individuals to fall in line, follow the rules, and support those in positions of authority. One of the main ways this influence is maintained is through communication.

In the end, the power of words and beliefs cannot be underestimated. What we speak into existence has a profound impact on our lives and the lives of those around us. Our words shape our perception of reality and reflect our inner selves. For this reason, it is important to be mindful of the words we choose, making sure they align with our beliefs and aspirations. By speaking life into ourselves and others, we help cultivate positivity and create the conditions for a prosperous and fulfilling life. Conversely, speaking death and negativity can lead us down a path of despair and unfulfilled desires.

Life is like a beast that feeds on whatever we give it. If we feed it negativity, drama, gossip, and a mindsct of lack, that is what it will thrive on. However, if we feed it positivity, hard work, affirmations, and presence, it can become a source of prosperity. Our words hold incredible power, and they can either uplift or tear down. It is up to us to choose our words wisely and use them to create a life filled with joy, abundance, and fulfillment.

Remember, whether you believe in something or not, belief itself carries power. When you believe you can achieve something, you are far more likely to succeed. Be mindful of the words you speak, because once spoken they cannot be taken back. They leave a lasting impact on others and shape how people perceive you. Speak life into yourself and into others, because what you speak has a way of shaping your reality. Embrace the power of words and use them to create a life that aligns with your dreams and aspirations.

# CHAPTER 37

## You Can't Hear Or See a Tree Grow

In the grand tapestry of life, one undeniable truth emerges: growth often goes unnoticed. Just as a tree begins as a small seed, our personal development unfolds gradually and often imperceptibly. Picture a young sapling in a vast forest. Each day it stands tall, appearing unchanged, yet beneath the surface its roots grow deeper and its trunk becomes stronger. If you visit that tree after a few months, you might not notice a dramatic difference. However, return after a year or two, and you will witness its transformation into a towering presence rising above the forest floor.

This metaphor captures the essence of change in our lives. Many people declare their intentions to change by setting New Year's resolutions or committing to new diets. Yet true transformation rarely happens overnight. It requires time, patience, and consistent effort. We must cultivate positive habits and nurture them like seeds so they can grow into lasting changes in our behavior.

To begin meaningful change, we must first examine and adjust our environment. Just as a tree requires sunlight, rain, and nutrients to thrive, we also depend on the conditions around us. Our environment shapes our thoughts, feelings, and ultimately our actions. By consciously choosing what we expose ourselves to, whether it is the media we consume, the conversations we engage in, or the people we surround ourselves with, we can guide our growth in a healthier direction.

The eyes are often described as the gateway to the soul, yet it is our ears that serve as the gateway to the mind. The words and sounds we absorb influence how we think, interpret situations, and respond to the world around us. By being selective about what we listen to, we can reshape our thinking and cultivate a more positive and disciplined mindset. This transformation doesn't come only from external influences. It also grows from the conversations we have with ourselves.

To genuinely embrace change, one must be willing to overhaul every aspect of life. This means reassessing relationships, removing toxic influences, and replacing negative thoughts from the past with positive affirmations. It involves adjusting our diet, reshaping our perspectives, and ultimately becoming the person we aspire to be.

Behavioral change, as understood by analysts, unfolds gradually over time. We cannot expect instant results from superficial adjustments. Instead, we must actively reshape the factors that influence our lives, reinforcing positive behaviors and encouraging the outcomes we desire. It is important to recognize that negative influences cannot coexist with positive aspirations. Simply put, you cannot continue feeding negativity into your life and expect to flourish.

Facing challenges head on is a vital part of personal growth. Avoidance rarely leads to progress. For example, if someone struggles with shyness around women, the solution is not retreating but gaining experience through interaction. Engaging with more people gradually reduces fear and builds confidence. The discomfort of rejection becomes a lesson in resilience and strength, allowing a person to approach future situations with greater confidence.

Many individuals believe that running away from their problems is a solution. In reality, avoidance often allows those problems to grow stronger. Like a fire that burns intensely, some fears must be confronted directly. The choice is simple. We can continue running from our challenges, or we can face them with courage and grow stronger because of it.

As we move through life, we must accept that growth doesn't always make the path easier. Consider the tree that perseveres against gravity, pests, and storms. It remains rooted and continues reaching toward the sky despite the obstacles it faces. This kind of resilience is essential for anyone who hopes to succeed, regardless of the circumstances or hardships they encounter.

The path to success is often marked by loss. Just as many celebrated boxers carry records filled with defeat, we too must accept our failures as part of our development. To become something new, we must often release what we once were. This idea appears in many philosophies, including the biblical concept that death can represent transformation and renewal.

In behavior analysis, the Fair Pair Rule reflects this same principle. To eliminate a behavior, it must be replaced with something constructive. An old habit cannot simply disappear without something else taking its place. If we do not consciously choose what fills that space, it may be replaced by something harmful.

As you reflect on your journey, remember that growth is often a solitary process. Few people witness transformation as it happens, so seeking constant validation from others will only distract you. Like a tree that quietly stretches toward the sun, your growth may remain unseen for a long time. Yet when you finally step forward after that period of development, others may hardly recognize the person you have become.

In this chapter we uncover an important truth. Growth is a quiet and deeply personal journey filled with challenges, lessons, and transformation. Embrace the process, nurture your roots, and trust that, like a mighty tree, your strength will flourish in time.

# CHAPTER 38
## Change Your Environment

In the grand tapestry of existence, our environment serves as the canvas upon which our lives are painted. Just as a flower requires sunlight and water, every living organism depends on an environment that supports its growth. In many ways, we are products of our surroundings. Our thoughts, ambitions, and even our identities are shaped by the spaces we inhabit. Yet how often do we pause to consider the profound influence our environments have on our potential?

Consider the caterpillar, a creature destined for transformation. Without the leaves that nourish it or the branches that provide stability, it cannot rise toward its potential as a butterfly. This metamorphosis serves as a powerful metaphor for our own lives. Many remarkable individuals, filled with talent and brilliance, remain hidden in the shadows simply because they exist in environments that do not support their growth. They may possess the ability to soar, yet their circumstances keep them grounded.

Stories of those who pursue the American dream often reveal this reality. We hear about individuals who rose from poverty and overcame tremendous obstacles to achieve success. Yet we rarely hear about those who possessed the same gifts but were restrained by the weight of their surroundings. It is a sobering thought that potential can wither when the conditions required for growth are absent.

Life is not static. It moves in cycles and constantly presents opportunities to adapt. When we find ourselves in environments that suffocate rather than support us, we have the ability to change our circumstances. Unlike plants or animals, we can consciously choose to seek environments that align with our ambitions. This choice is not simply a luxury. For those who wish to grow and flourish, it is a necessity.

Migration is a natural phenomenon that occurs not only among birds but throughout the spectrum of life. Birds instinctively move toward environments that support their survival. They understand that comfort can become the enemy of growth. In the same way, we must accept the discomfort that often accompanies change if we hope to reach our full potential. The choice is ours. We can remain in familiar surroundings that slowly erode our confidence and sense of worth, or we can venture into the unknown, much like a caterpillar emerging from its cocoon into the vibrant world of butterflies.

To truly thrive, we must surround ourselves with people who inspire and challenge us. The company we keep has a powerful influence on the direction of our lives. Ask yourself an honest question. Are you the brightest star in your circle? If so, it may be time to search for new constellations. Complacency, like stagnant water, produces little growth. We often become the average of the five people with whom we spend the most time. If those around us are satisfied with mediocrity, we risk becoming another link in that same cycle of stagnation. Instead, seek individuals who stretch your limits and encourage your development.

In the journey of life, expansion is the language of the universe. It is a force that constantly pushes life forward, while stagnation quietly leads to decay. Embracing the unfamiliar can be intimidating, yet it opens the door to countless possibilities. Every new environment offers a fresh perspective, a chance to rediscover your voice, and an opportunity to shine among those who recognize and appreciate your unique gifts.

Beware of the crabs in the bucket, those who pull you back down as you strive to rise. Their love may be genuine, yet it is often rooted in fear. They may resist your success because it disrupts their comfort or challenges the limits they have placed on themselves. Love them, but understand their limitations. Your journey belongs to you alone, and while they may walk beside you for a time, your path may lead to heights they cannot yet imagine.

Listen to your intuition. It is a compass that guides you toward environments that support your growth. A rose cannot bloom in a harsh desert, just as you cannot thrive in a space that stifles your spirit. The road ahead may hold challenges, but it is also filled with opportunities for transformation. Have the courage to seek out the places that resonate with your purpose, where you can grow and flourish like the vibrant bloom you were meant to become.

In the end, the question remains. Are you ready to change your environment and embrace the full beauty of your potential? The choice is yours. Choose wisely, because the journey of self discovery often begins with the spaces we choose to inhabit.

# CHAPTER 39

## The Equivalence Law: Pain=Pleasure

As a young child, I had a very clear mission: avoid pain at all costs. I wanted nothing to do with sadness, gossip, or deceit. In my mind, the ideal world was filled with sunshine and roses, a place where hurt was nothing more than a myth, like unicorns or a friendly encounter with the neighborhood raccoon. Spoiler alert: that world doesn't exist.

The more I tried to dodge pain, the more it seemed to hunt me down like a determined game warden with a personal vendetta. Let me be honest. I struggled with serious self-esteem issues growing up. I came from a loving family in College Park, and from the outside things looked good. My friends called us "the hustlers" and joked that we were rich. In reality, our wealth had more to do with structured living than gold-plated toilets. They never saw the inner workings of my life.

By the time I was eight, my siblings had already left for college. I found myself alone in a house that often felt more like an empty library than a home. I was the last child, but in many ways I also felt like the only child.

With my parents working tirelessly, I spent most of my time with my grandmother. She was sweet in many ways, but she also had a darker side. Life had dealt her some difficult hands, and instead of using those experiences to uplift others, she often projected her pain onto me. I remember one moment when she warned me that if I didn't wash my hands I would get AIDS. Yes, that is not how it works, but try explaining that to an eight-year-old.

Her version of affection often came with a running commentary. "You're a nasty, smelly boy," she would say, knocking on my door like the most persistent door-to-door salesperson in history. "When are you going to get a girlfriend? Are you gay?" For a child already struggling with self-image, those words cut deeper than any blade. I didn't know how to talk to girls, and I certainly didn't understand the importance of health or hygiene yet. But does anyone ever tell a developing mind that it's not okay to throw shade?

Yet here's the twist: through all that pain, I found strength. My parents didn't realize the extent of my struggles until much later, and when I told them, they apologized. But I waved it off. My grandmother was the best thing that ever happened to me, despite the verbal punches. Her harsh words forged me like a sword in fire. Diamonds, after all, are formed under pressure.

I've faced pressure from many directions: a football coach who once predicted I'd amount to nothing, neighborhood kids calling me an idiot, and college roommates who turned my home into a Trap house. There was even a divorce that sent me spiraling into the depths of depression, drugs, and alcohol. But through it all, I learned a fundamental truth: pain equals pleasure.

If you're willing to confront the uncomfortable, you'll discover insights that most people never see. Many people avoid pain like it's a bad smell in the gym locker room, but the truth is that embracing it can take you to extraordinary places.

Take my battle with weight, for example. Being overweight felt good, like wrapping myself in a cozy blanket of mediocrity. But guess what? That comfort also pointed toward a shorter life and deeper self esteem issues. So I hit the gym. The pain of running, lifting weights, and sweating buckets taught me discipline and consistency. Over time it transformed me into the gladiator I am today.

People often ask me, "How did you get so fit?" The answer is simple: I welcomed pain and came out the other side with pleasure.

Now let's talk about the flip side of this equation. Pleasure can equal pain too. Fun, as it turns out, can be overrated. You might think a night out drinking is harmless entertainment, but that same night could leave you in jail or dealing with a paternity suit from someone you barely remember. What begins as fun can quickly slide into debauchery once adulthood gets involved.

As kids, we play. As adults, we vacation. The difference is that many adults mistake indulgence for happiness. Excessive pleasure often carries a hidden cost. Too much partying leads to hangovers, poor decisions, and regrets that linger longer than the fun ever did. But when you flip the script and accept the pain of discipline, whether that means grinding in the gym or putting in extra hours at work, you eventually step into a version of yourself that feels far closer to heaven.

Life is about growth, and growth requires endurance. Just as a seed must be buried in dark, damp soil before it can sprout, we must pass through difficulty before we can flourish. Pain is not always the enemy. If you allow it, pain becomes a teacher.

In the end, you cannot control everything that happens to you, but you can control how you interpret it. Life is still good. If it were not, God would have pressed the delete button on the whole experiment by now. So stop complaining about the struggles around you and embrace the discomfort. Stand up, face your pain, and turn it into your greatest ally on the path to real pleasure.

**Key Takeaways:**

- Pain is a necessary part of growth.
- Embracing discomfort leads to transformation.
- True fulfillment requires a balance between pleasure and pain.

So ask yourself one simple question. Are you ready to face the pain that leads to your pleasure?

# CHAPTER 40
## The More You Do, The More You Get Done

As a kid, I used to think success was like a lottery. Some people were simply lucky, blessed with talent, while others were left standing out in the cold. It wasn't until I got older that I began to understand the truth. Success isn't just about luck or talent. It's about the relentless effort you put in. The more you do, the more you accomplish.

Let me share a story that made this lesson real for me. Growing up, I dreamed of playing in the NFL. I had the skills. I was a first-string player and consistently showed flashes of talent. But for reasons I didn't fully understand at the time, the coaches never viewed me as the standout I believed I was.

Meanwhile, I had a friend who eventually became an NFL Hall of Famer. One night I was throwing a party and enjoying life when he showed up early. I joked with him about arriving before the fun even started. He calmly told me that his mom had given him a curfew. He had to be home by 11.

At the time, I couldn't wrap my mind around it. I didn't understand how someone could still have fun while dedicating so much time to training, running drills, sharpening his skills, and keeping his grades up. Looking back, the difference between us became clear.

It wasn't that he was more talented than I was. It was the commitment he made to his craft. It took me years to understand that lesson. For a long time I searched for shortcuts and chose fun over discipline. Eventually reality caught up with me. If I truly wanted to achieve my dreams, I had to put in the work.

Now I wake up at 4 AM to work out and tackle my tasks before the day even begins. Starting early gives me an advantage. I've also learned that making lists and completing tasks improves my productivity. The truth is simple. You must be willing to do what others won't if you want to have what others don't. When you invest your time and energy into self improvement, you build resilience. You learn to face life's challenges head on, which makes you stronger and better prepared for whatever comes your way.

Think of life like lifting weights. At first the struggle is real. It's difficult, and you may feel like giving up. But with persistence you grow stronger and healthier. Life works the same way. When you commit to reaching your full potential every day, even small actions contribute to your growth. Simple tasks like making your bed can build discipline. I often tell my daughter, "If you can't handle the small things, how can you handle the big challenges?"

Many people complain about their struggles and wait for someone to come rescue them. But how can you expect to receive when you haven't invested in yourself? None of this is easy, and I won't pretend that it is. Success requires time, effort, and patience. After all, Rome wasn't built in a day.

When I pursued my board certification, I faced numerous obstacles. My past mistakes followed me, and life was far from easy. At one point I was even wearing an ankle monitor. Still, I committed myself to studying every single day. Despite the circumstances, I refused to quit.

If you take away one principle from this chapter, let it be this: work hard now and life will become easier later. If you choose to play now, you may find yourself paying the price later. Life is built on choices, and every decision leads to consequences. Some will be good and others will be difficult. When you prioritize self improvement and focus on what truly matters, the rewards eventually follow. When you procrastinate and avoid responsibility, the consequences of inaction will catch up to you.

Life can be tedious, and it is not always entertaining, but the work is necessary. If you are unwilling to put in the effort, you will likely settle for a mediocre existence. Dreams do not simply appear out of nowhere. They require planning, execution, and resilience. Anyone who has achieved their dreams will tell you the same thing. The path was never easy.

Failure is often a prerequisite for success. You may fail 99% of the time, but that 1% of success can change everything.

What many people fail to realize is that failure can be more valuable than success. Through failure we learn, adapt, and grow stronger. No one enjoys failing, yet it remains an essential part of the journey. God doesn't always grant our desires in the form of blessings. Sometimes those blessings arrive as lessons. Victory feels far more meaningful when it's earned through struggle.

So keep pushing forward. As Sylvester Stallone wrote for the character Rocky Balboa, "That's how winning is done." The same principle applies to the choices we make every day. If you choose to prioritize partying and indulgence, understand that life has a way of holding you accountable. Sacrifice is often the price of achievement.

Change is one of life's greatest gifts. Many people resist it, but without change nothing in nature would grow. Flowers would never bloom, and storms would never give way to sunlight. Embrace the balance of life and remember this simple truth. The more you do, the more you accomplish.

**The Law of Choice**

In the grand tapestry of life, one thread stands out above the rest: the power of choice. It is a curious idea. Some people argue that our paths are already mapped out, predetermined by some cosmic force. Others, like myself, believe firmly in the freedom to steer our own ships. God did not create a world where we are merely puppets dancing to the whims of fate. Instead, He gave us the extraordinary gift of choice. With that gift comes the ability to change our direction, reshape our lives, and sometimes even influence the world around us.

Now let's be honest for a moment. Humans are a perplexing species. We can be selfish, destructive, and sometimes downright ridiculous, almost like a colony of bacteria determined to disrupt everything in its path. While animals move through life guided by instinct, we carry the burden and privilege of opinion. That ability to choose is what truly sets us apart. We can choose our perspectives, our paths, and even the people we surround ourselves with.

Take my friend Byron as an example. Byron was a genius in disguise. He could sell ice to an Eskimo, pitch kryptonite to Superman, and turn something as simple as a donut into a profitable business. Byron had the mind of a natural entrepreneur. He was destined for greatness, but only if he chose the right path.

One night he came down to college for a party and ended up making more than a thousand dollars selling donuts and CDs. It was impressive to watch. But like many brilliant minds caught in the web of temptation, he became drawn to the quick money that came with selling drugs.

Byron had the instincts of a true businessman, but his choices pulled him into a cycle of trouble. He spent more time dealing with the law than building the empire he was capable of creating. I remember producing music with him when he was on the verge of something big. His talent was undeniable. Yet just as things started to take off, he was pulled over again with a trunk full of problems.

Life, my friends, ultimately comes down to choices. You can go left or you can go right, but every direction carries a consequence.

God gave us the freedom to choose our paths, but with that freedom comes responsibility. Making the right choice is rarely easy. In many cases, doing the right thing offers no immediate reward, while the wrong choice delivers instant gratification. This is what makes temptation so powerful. The excitement of a night out or the rush that comes from quick money may feel rewarding in the moment, but the consequences eventually catch up.

This cycle can be especially harsh in underserved communities, where many young people lack the guidance needed to see the full range of their options. They look at their circumstances and think, "By any means, I must escape this." Unfortunately, instead of pursuing education or learning vocational skills, many turn toward illegal activities. In doing so, they unintentionally continue a cycle that has affected generations. It's a systemic issue with deep historical roots, particularly in Black communities where long periods of oppression have left lasting scars.

Yet there is still a powerful truth within all of this. You have the ability to break free from the grip of history. History is often described as "His story," but your life is your story. Each day you write a new chapter, and every decision you make becomes the ink on the page.

Of course, it's often easier to remain in a bad relationship or maintain friendships that no longer benefit you. But easy decisions frequently lead to deeper problems. The difficult choices, leaving a toxic relationship, pursuing a demanding career path, or distancing yourself from negative influences, often produce the most meaningful growth. Life contains a strange paradox. The hardest choices are often the right ones, while the easiest choices can quietly lead us in the wrong direction.

As my father always said, "There's nothing good about being poor." Poverty is not just a matter of money. In many ways, it's a mindset. True wealth comes from the richness of your experiences, the strength of your relationships, and the ability to come home to people who fill your life with joy.

Do not fall into the trap of systemic deprivation. Value your heart, make your own choices, and remember that every decision carries weight. Your next choice could shape the rest of your life. Think of life as a lobby filled with doors. Each door represents a different choice, and every choice leads to a different room. Choose wisely, and you may find yourself stepping into a place filled with love, success, and fulfillment.

So step boldly into the lobby of life. Embrace your freedom to choose, because within that freedom lies the power to shape your destiny. In the end, it's not just a story being written. It's your life, and you hold the pen.

**The Law of Behavior**

Writing this chapter feels like stepping into a world I know intimately, yet one that remains endlessly complex: the world of behavior. As a Board Certified Behavior Analyst, my work centers on analyzing behavior, identifying patterns, and applying behavioral principles to create meaningful change.

Entire libraries have been written about the science of Applied Behavior Analysis. If the subject interests you, I encourage you to explore the research. For now, my goal is simpler. I want to introduce the core ideas that anyone can understand and apply, regardless of their background.

At the center of behavioral analysis are four primary functions of behavior: attention, sensory stimulation, tangible rewards, and escape. These four functions explain why any organism behaves the way it does. Understanding them is essential for anyone who wants to influence behavior, change habits, or better understand the actions of others.

**Attention**

Let's begin with the force that drives much of human interaction: attention. Some might argue that money is the greatest motivator in life, but I contend that attention reigns supreme. We are social creatures, wired to seek validation and recognition. In today's world, that desire has only intensified, especially with the rise of social media. Platforms built to capture and monetize our attention have reshaped how we interact and often encourage behavior that prioritizes visibility over substance.

Consider how early this dynamic begins. Take a baby, for example. When an infant cries, it's not merely a sound. It's a primal signal for attention and a request for nourishment, comfort, or care. For many people, this instinct never fully disappears. Instead, it evolves. Adults may not cry in the same way, but they often seek attention through other behaviors such as dramatic reactions, constant messaging, or relentless posting on social media.

If you want to change attention-seeking behavior, the key is differential reinforcement. In simple terms, this means refusing to reward the behaviors you don't want to see. Instead, direct your attention toward the behaviors you want to encourage. Consider a common example: a partner who bombards you with calls and texts when they're upset. Responding immediately may unintentionally reinforce the behavior. A more effective approach is to communicate clear boundaries and let them know that you'll engage when the conversation becomes respectful or calm. Over time, this shifts the incentive structure that drives their behavior.

I see similar patterns in the workplace. Adults aren't immune to negative attention-seeking. When someone approaches me with persistent negativity through texts, calls, or conversations, I intentionally redirect the discussion or withdraw my attention altogether. By doing so, I avoid reinforcing the drama and instead reward more constructive interaction.

The principle is simple but powerful. Attention functions as a kind of currency. Where you invest it determines which behaviors grow stronger. Learning to manage that currency wisely can profoundly shape the quality of your relationships.

## Tangible Rewards

Next, we have tangible rewards. These are the physical items or benefits people seek, such as money, cars, or status symbols. In many ways, our society is driven by these pursuits. This is particularly evident in relationships where individuals chase material gains or remain in situations that are not healthy simply because of the tangible benefits they receive.

Withholding tangible rewards until you see the desired behavior can be a powerful motivator. This principle appears across many areas of life, from parenting to workplace dynamics. If you want someone to change their behavior, make sure the reward is clearly tied to their actions. When people understand that positive outcomes depend on what they do, they're more likely to adjust their behavior.

For instance, in relationships, withholding physical affection until positive behaviors are displayed can encourage change. When rewards are contingent on respectful or constructive behavior, they become a powerful tool for shaping how people act.

## Sensory Stimulation

The third function involves sensory stimulation. These are the pleasurable sensations that enrich our experiences and make certain activities rewarding. Humans are naturally drawn to experiences that provide sensory input, whether through touch, taste, sound, or other sensations. Because of this, sensory experiences can strongly influence motivation and behavior.

When you want to encourage certain behaviors, think about how sensory stimulation can serve as a reward. If someone responds well to sensory input, providing that feedback when they demonstrate the desired behavior can reinforce those actions. This approach works with both children and adults who are motivated by sensory experiences.

## Escape

Lastly, we have escape, which often appears in the form of avoidance behavior. This occurs when individuals try to evade situations or tasks that feel unpleasant, stressful, or anxiety-inducing. For example, if I know there's traffic, I might take a shortcut to avoid the hassle. This instinct is natural. Most people prefer to escape discomfort whenever possible.

To address escape behaviors effectively, it's important to set clear expectations. For instance, if you have an employee who frequently calls in sick, you may need to clarify that consistent attendance is required to maintain their position. When expectations are clearly communicated, individuals often adjust their behavior to avoid negative consequences.

## Reinforcement vs. Punishment

Understanding these four functions of behavior helps us recognize that behavior is not inherently good or bad. It simply exists as a response to various stimuli. Reinforcement increases desirable behaviors, while punishment attempts to decrease undesirable ones. The real challenge lies in how these strategies are applied.

Parents, for example, often focus heavily on punishment. They may scold children for their mistakes while overlooking opportunities to reinforce positive behavior. This imbalance can create a cycle in which children feel discouraged and unrecognized for their efforts.

Instead, we should aim to reinforce good behavior more frequently than we punish bad behavior. When positive actions receive attention and acknowledgment, they are more likely to be repeated.

Imagine a child who is consistently reprimanded for misbehavior but rarely acknowledged for their accomplishments. Over time, that child may begin to associate attention primarily with negativity. This pattern can reduce motivation and discourage positive behavior.

The better approach is to celebrate successes, even small ones, while addressing mistakes in a constructive and supportive way.

**The Law of Behavior**

In conclusion, the Law of Behavior is more than a theoretical construct; it's a practical framework that shapes every interaction and experience. By understanding the four functions of behavior (attention, tangible rewards, sensory stimulation, and escape), you gain insight into what motivates people. With that knowledge, you can influence behavior positively, whether in personal relationships, professional settings, or your own life.

Behavior is not merely something to analyze; it's a fundamental aspect of human existence. Mastering these principles helps you create a more harmonious environment for yourself and those around you. Ultimately, understanding behavior is not just a skill; it's a pathway to meaningful connections and transformative change.

**The Law of Organization**

"If you fail to plan, you plan to fail." This timeless adage echoes the wisdom of those who have walked the road to success. Life is a whirlwind of tasks, responsibilities, and distractions; without a firm grasp on organization, we risk becoming spectators in our own lives. Imagine navigating a maze without a map; frustration mounts and progress stalls. Armed with a plan, however, you can chart a clear course through the chaos, turning your journey from overwhelming to purposeful.

Let's face it: prioritization can be daunting. When a million things vie for your attention, it is easy to feel overwhelmed. Yet dedicating time to prepare before tackling any task can boost your chances of success by a remarkable 85%. That figure is not just a statistic; it is a life-altering insight. Whether you are a student cramming for exams, a professional juggling deadlines, or a parent managing daily chaos, having a game plan is essential.

Consider the world of sports: without coaches guiding players, we would see a cluster of individuals running aimlessly, each trying to score without any cohesion or strategy. Coaches supply the blueprint—the plan that positions athletes for success. Likewise, in life, strategy outweighs sheer action. You can run around like a headless chicken, but without clear direction you will only exhaust yourself and achieve nothing meaningful.

Chess offers a vivid example of strategy at work. Every piece has a defined role, and victory belongs to the player who anticipates several moves in advance, placing each piece with purpose. The same discipline applies to life: when you cultivate the habit of planning, you build consistency, develop discipline, and learn to approach tasks with a clear mindset.

One of the most effective ways to manage work is to "eat the frog," meaning you tackle the hardest task first. This tactic clears mental clutter and sets a productive tone for the day. By confronting the most challenging item at the outset, you can move through the rest of your to-do list methodically, free from the weight of procrastination. Think of the day as a battlefield; the victor is the one who arrives prepared with a strategy. Gaining momentum over your opponent, whether that opponent is a deadline, a project, or a daunting chore, requires having the right pieces in place.

To illustrate this point, consider an analogy involving the sun. The sun radiates warmth and light, nurturing life without causing harm. However, when that sunlight passes through a magnifying glass, the energy converges on a single point and can ignite a flame. The same principle of concentration and focus is vital to achieving your goals. By directing your energy toward a specific task or set of tasks, you create a powerful force that produces results.

A practical way to channel this focus is by creating lists. Writing down each task you need to accomplish not only helps you remember it but also instills a sense of accountability. Benjamin Franklin, one of history's most prolific figures, mastered this technique. He meticulously drafted lists for holidays, tasks, and goals. If he did not complete an item, he carried it over to the next day, ensuring nothing slipped through the cracks. This simple act of organization gave him a decisive advantage over his peers and contributed to his remarkable success.

Today, we can use a variety of organizational tools and techniques to streamline our lives. The Eisenhower Matrix, for example, helps you sort tasks by urgency and importance. By categorizing your responsibilities into four quadrants (urgent and important; important but not urgent; urgent but not important; and neither), you gain clarity about what to tackle first. This method empowers you to focus on high-priority tasks while delegating or postponing less critical ones.

Now, let's get real about daily life. I have found that taking time to prepare on Sundays is a game changer. I meal-prep for the week, ensuring I have healthy, ready-to-eat options at my fingertips. This simple habit spares me the daily drudgery of cooking and frees me to focus on other important tasks. I also map out my weekly schedule, outlining what must be done, much like a general preparing for battle.

By strategically prioritizing my tasks, first handling the most important ones and leaving smaller, less impactful items for later, I create a sense of order amid chaos. The system is not always perfect, but even when I fall short, I know that without planning I would be adrift in a sea of disorder.

The beauty of organization is that it breeds confidence. When you have a plan, you are not merely reacting to life's challenges; you are navigating them with purpose. This proactive stance builds momentum and reinforces a cycle of achievement that elevates your mental and emotional well-being.

Ultimately, organization is a fundamental factor that separates the highly accomplished from the rest. By taking time to plan and organize, you give yourself the best chance of success, becoming the master of your own destiny and tackling life's challenges with clarity and purpose.

So, as you move forward in life, remember the power of planning and organization. Embrace the process, and let it guide you toward your goals. A well-organized life is not just about checking off tasks; it's about creating the life you desire, one thoughtful decision at a time. Organization is not merely a skill; it's a way of life that can turn your journey into a purposeful and fulfilling adventure.

**Law of In and Out**

**You are what you attract; you must become what you desire**

You are what you attract. This mantra captures the essence of our existence. The people who enter our lives, the opportunities we encounter, and even our personal successes all reflect who we are on the inside. Think of the familiar saying, "you are what you eat." If you consume junk, your body shows it in both health and energy. Likewise, if you do not embody the qualities you want, you will not draw them toward you.

Let's break this down. Suppose you want a partner who is loyal, nurturing, and supportive. First cultivate those same qualities within yourself. You cannot expect to meet someone who radiates integrity and kindness if you are not actively working to be a good person. It is a simple equation: your internal state must align with your external desires.

We often notice seemingly perfect pairs: the drug dealer with the stripper, the millionaire with the artist, the athlete with the creative type. Although opposites can attract, they frequently share a chaotic energy that shows up in their relationships. Take Kanye West and Kim Kardashian, for instance. Whatever your opinion of their personalities, both are complex individuals, and their partnership reflected that complexity. Crazy recognizes crazy; it's like a magnet pulling together similar energies.

If you are selfish, looking out only for yourself, do you honestly think you will attract someone humble and generous? Absolutely not. You will draw in a partner who mirrors your chaos—perhaps a drama-seeker who slashes your tires or a toxic companion who thrives on conflict.

Life has a remarkable way of projecting your inner state onto the outside world. Seldom do you meet someone whose outer beauty is not matched by inner depth. I have met stunning women whose personalities were as toxic as they were captivating, and they attracted partners who exploited those traits.

What is the takeaway? Align your core values with your aspirations. If you want wealth, you cannot keep a poverty mindset. If you desire health, you must shed unhealthy habits. Transformation begins within. If you are a rat on the inside, you will appear as one on the outside. If you are a stallion on the inside, your confidence and strength will shine through.

The principle is straightforward: life favors those who embody what they desire. This idea echoes the biblical declaration "I am who I am." It is more than a catchy phrase; it affirms the power of self-awareness. Your actions, decisions, and outcomes flow from the core of who you are.

If you want to change your surroundings, begin by changing yourself. Want to be rich? Imitate the habits of wealthy people. Most successful individuals rise at dawn, exercise regularly, and devote weekends to growth instead of partying. They reject the lure of instant gratification in favor of long-term gains.

Bad habits eventually catch up with you, just as good habits compound over time. These are not empty words; they are universal laws. I have experienced this myself. I was not always the person I am today, and my mistakes drew people who mirrored my flaws. I accepted being used because I sought companionship among those who were equally adrift.

Life teaches hard lessons. The consequences of your actions may be delayed, but they always return. This is karma in motion, a pattern that mirrors the choices we make. Negative behavior reinforces negative patterns until disaster strikes, whereas positive choices generate positive results.

Consider celebrities who seem to evade accountability. Their wealth may shield them for a time, yet the truth eventually surfaces. Look at figures such as Jeffrey Epstein or others embroiled in scandal after scandal. Their past actions, whether they believed they could outrun them or not, always catch up.

Be mindful, then, of every decision. Each choice sends ripples that return in ways you may not expect. The Law of In and Out reminds us that we are what we attract; if we persist in foolishness, we will continue to draw foolishness into our lives.

In the end, everything comes down to self-awareness. Reflect on who you are and who you want to become, then align your actions with your aspirations. The universe often provides what you need, yet you must first grow into the person who can receive it. Life is a mirror; what you see is usually a reflection of yourself. Cultivate your character wisely, and the world around you will respond in kind.

## Stacking Wins

On the journey of personal growth and achievement, the idea of "stacking wins" stands out as a powerful strategy. Lasting progress is not about competing with others; it's about surpassing your own performance each day. Your most formidable opponent is the self-doubt and complacency lurking within, so aim to outdo your inner critic daily.

Stacking wins involves accumulating small, manageable victories that build on one another. A win can be as simple as making your bed, arriving at work on time, or completing a daily workout. Each action, however minor, strengthens your discipline and sense of accomplishment. Remember that both wins and losses compound over time; neglecting small tasks can create setbacks that slow your progress.

Just as a house is built brick by brick, personal growth is achieved through consistent, incremental efforts. It's not about reaching monumental goals overnight, but about laying a solid foundation with everyday actions. This approach not only keeps you motivated but also prepares you for bigger challenges ahead.

Many people struggle to achieve their goals because they never get started. Focusing on small habits, like keeping your space tidy or choosing healthier foods, lays the groundwork for larger accomplishments. Conversely, stacking losses can trigger a downward spiral, so it's crucial to commit to stacking wins instead.

Engaging in physical activity is another vital aspect of stacking wins. Regular workouts do more than improve your appearance; they train your mind to embrace challenges and build resilience. The gym serves as a powerful metaphor for life: the effort you invest directly correlates with the results you achieve. Excuses hold no weight, because the gym reflects reality and reveals both your strengths and areas for improvement.

Real growth comes from embracing the process. Nothing worth having comes easily, and the lessons learned through hard work are invaluable. Just as lottery winners often end up broke because they didn't earn their wealth, you need to cultivate the skills and values required to sustain success.

Life is about nurturing your potential, much like tending a seed that will grow into a strong tree. It takes time and effort, yet the rewards endure. Each day offers an opportunity to stack wins, no matter how small, creating a compounding effect that opens the door to new possibilities.

Remember, the days you choose not to show up could be the turning points in your life. Don't let those opportunities slip away. Embrace each day with the intention of stacking your wins, and watch how they accumulate to transform your future.

# CHAPTER 41
## The Law Of The Gym

Let's talk about the gym, and no, it's not just the place with sweat-soaked mats and the occasional rogue smell of protein shakes gone bad. It's a sanctuary, a sacred ground where the battle for your mind and body takes place. Before you roll your eyes and think, "Oh great, another fitness guru," hear me out. This isn't just about bulging biceps or chiseled abs; it's about cultivating discipline, and that's where the real magic happens.

**Motivation vs. Discipline**

Let's break it down. Motivation is like that friend who promises to help you move but mysteriously disappears when it's time to lift boxes. It's fleeting, unpredictable, and, quite frankly, a bit of a flake. One day you're pumped up, ready to conquer the world; the next you're binge-watching cat videos on YouTube. Discipline, on the other hand, is the steadfast partner who shows up every day, rain or shine, ready to tackle the hard stuff. It doesn't care how you feel; it's all about consistency and persistence.

Think of discipline as the reliable old car that gets you to work each day, while motivation is that shiny sports car you can't afford and only see circling the block once a month.

**The Gym: Your Secret Weapon**

Why the gym? Because it's the ultimate training ground for life. Feeling down? Go to the gym. Happy? Go to the gym. Need a miracle? You guessed it, go to the gym. It's not just a place to build muscle; it's where you build character. When I step inside,

I'm not only trying to look good in a swimsuit (though that's a nice bonus); I'm there to win the battle in my head.

Every time I drag myself to the gym, I'm lifting more than weights; I'm lifting my spirits. If I can silence the voice that says, "You're too tired," I've already won the day. Here's the kicker: your mind has to lead the way. When it decides, "We're doing this," your body has no choice but to follow.

## The Ritual of Hard Work

Let's be real: getting out of bed is often harder than the workout itself. Many people skip the gym because they'd rather snuggle deeper into their blankets. But here's the truth: the gym gives you a sense of accomplishment that echoes throughout your day. It becomes a rhythm, a pattern of success.

I remember going through my divorce and grappling with addiction. Everyone has battles, some more visible than others, but for me, hitting the gym was crucial. It conditioned my mind to believe that everything would be okay. Every rep, every set, was a promise to myself that I was getting better, one day at a time.

## No Gym? No Problem!

And hey, let's not be elitist about this gym thing. Not everyone can afford a membership, nor do they need one. You can work out at home, do yoga, meditate, or even focus on deep breathing. It all contributes to building that mental fortress. When you strengthen your mind, everything else falls into place.

## The Devil's Playground: Laziness

In our society, laziness is like that annoying little gremlin that keeps whispering, "Just one more episode." It's easy to fall into the trap of wishing and hoping for a better life while doing nothing about it. But dreams don't come true by lounging around; they're forged in the fire of action.

The gym is the perfect starting point. Not only does it condition your body, but it also boosts your energy levels. When you're in shape, you tackle life with gusto. Your mind and body start to synchronize, and suddenly you're a well-oiled machine ready to take on the world.

**The Art of Sacrifice**

Now, here's where it gets serious. To receive, you must first give. That means sacrificing comforts today for the benefit of your future. If you want to provide for your family, safeguard your health, and handle your business, you have to tackle the hard stuff now.

Look at legends like Mike Tyson, Kobe Bryant, and Michael Jordan. They didn't earn greatness by partying every night. Sure, a little fun is fine, but let's face it, fun is overrated when it comes to real success. Progress demands grit and determination.

**The Gym as a Life Lesson**

If you ever lack motivation, feel stuck, or just don't want to do anything, do yourself a favor and lift some weights. The weights don't care about excuses; they show you who you really are. Once you get in shape, you gain confidence, validation that comes from yourself, not from others.

Remember, the gym isn't just a physical space; it reflects how you're doing in life. It teaches you that, yes, it's hard, and yes, you'll want to quit sometimes. But as long as you keep pushing, you learn that you can accomplish anything, even in tough times.

So, when the alarm goes off in the morning, don't hit snooze. It starts with a single decision: get up and go. Sometimes just showing up is half the battle. Each workout is a step toward becoming the person you want to be.

I'll be honest; I don't always want to go to the gym. There are days when my couch calls my name louder than a siren. But it's a promise I made to myself. The hard things in life often deliver the best rewards, and choosing to do the hard stuff every day is what separates the average from the extraordinary.

So here's my advice: embrace the sanctuary of the gym. It's not just about shaping your body; it's about crafting your character. A strong mind and body form the ultimate duo in the game of life.

## The Sword Analogy

Let's embark on a journey together. Picture life as the crafting of a finely honed sword. To make that blade, you must place the steel in the fire, heating it enough to strengthen it without melting it into a puddle of disappointment.

## The Divine Lesson

In this story, a man learns from God that life mirrors the process of sharpening a sword. He grabs a dull blade, more butter knife than weapon, and places it in the fire, hoping to transform it. Then he asks, "How will I know when the sword is ready?"

God replies, "When you see my reflection in the sword." The message is clear: our struggles, hard times, and the fires of adversity are essential to growth. The situations that feel unbearable are the very moments that make us sharper, stronger, and more resilient.

## Embracing Hard Times

Life can be a roller-coaster ride without seatbelts, thrilling yet terrifying. The blessings we seek often arrive disguised as hardships. Those moments that test and hurt us are the ones that sharpen our metaphorical swords.

Consider the trials of Jesus or the story of Job. Job lost everything, including his family, wealth, and health, yet he remained steadfast in faith and was ultimately rewarded many times over. To embody a divine spirit, we have to withstand the heat, just like the sword forged in fire.

**The Practice of Life**

Life is like sports: you might have raw talent, but without hard work and dedication you'll finish in last place. You have to endure grueling practices, accept tough love from your coach, and push through pain. Losing isn't the end; it's simply a stepping stone on the road to victory.

I remember struggling with a test that most people breezed through. I could've wallowed in self-pity, but instead I treated each failure as a lesson. Every attempt taught me something valuable, and eventually I passed. That experience set me on a path that has given me ten times more than I ever imagined. I realized my struggles weren't a measure of my worth; they were part of God sharpening me for something greater.

**Appreciating the Struggles**

Sometimes we need to step back and appreciate the "bad stuff." Without rough patches we wouldn't recognize the good ones. If life were all roses it would lose its flavor. The fulfillment that comes from working hard, pushing through adversity, and finally succeeding is what makes the journey worthwhile.

So the next time you feel down, remember the sword analogy. The heat you're experiencing is simply a tool in the hands of a higher power, helping you uncover your true self. The reflection you seek isn't found in ease but in the strength forged through challenge.

In the end, like that sword, you'll emerge sharper, stronger, and ready for whatever life sends your way. Embrace the fire and let it reveal the warrior within.

# CHAPTER 42

## Not Everybody Is Made For You

L et's get one thing straight: not everyone in this vast universe, with more than four billion people and counting, was designed to be your bestie or confidant. Some folks are like seasonal outfits; they work for a while, then no longer fit. When you strive to elevate your life, not everyone around you will help you reach that goal. Some people arrive to teach lessons, while others turn out to be temporary distractions.

**The Crabs in the Bucket**

I once had a friend who shone like a shooting star but lived among "crabs in a bucket." Whenever she tried to climb higher, someone grabbed her ankles and pulled her back down. She was caring and nurturing, the kind who'd give you the shirt off her back, yet she attracted people who drained her energy instead of supporting her dreams.

She often said, "I just want to help everyone!" and I reminded her that you can't pour from an empty cup. The word *selfish* has become a dirty label, but let's redefine it: if you don't take care of yourself first, you can't take care of anyone else.

Picture inviting friends over only to watch them guzzle your alcohol and smoke your weed while you're left cleaning up afterward. One of her friends, a professional user, would leave her kids at home just to score a free meal, and her brother brought more drama than a soap opera, spreading emotional chaos wherever he went.

**The Math of Relationships**

This isn't just friendship; it's math. As I mentioned in a previous chapter, life is about adding and subtracting. If your friends keep chipping away at your happiness and goals, they're dragging you into complacency. You can't rise with people who are content to stay in the mud.

It's simple: if your circle is filled with negativity, you'll end up knee-deep in middle-ground misery. Rejection is part of life, and it's not a measure of your worth. Even the hottest celebrity hears "no." Every refusal is really a redirection, the universe handing you a litmus test to find the right path, or the right people.

**The Importance of Supportive People**

You deserve people who add value to your life, not energy vampires who drain you at every turn. Picture this: you're trying to pull yourself up, yet instead of encouragement, you get hands pulling you back down.

To find the right people, you first have to become the right person. Growth often brings loneliness; it signals that you're shedding old skin to make room for new growth. We all pass through seasons of isolation, but that feeling is a vital part of the journey.

**The Law of Self-Discovery**

You are here on this Earth to become the best version of yourself. Forget trying to mold someone into your ideal friend or partner. If you have a friend whose kids don't even respect them, what makes you think they'll respect you? It's like trying to build a house on quicksand; without a solid foundation, collapse is inevitable.

Even if you're the most talented, wealthy, or brilliant person alive, someone somewhere will still reject you. That's just life, so don't beat yourself up over it. See every rejection or tough decision to leave a situation as a stepping stone toward growth.

Perspective is everything. If you view rejection as a closed door instead of a detour, you'll miss new opportunities and experiences. Embrace the fact that not everyone is made for you, and that's perfectly okay. The right people will show up when you're ready, and they'll help you shine even brighter.

So let those seasonal friends drift away. Focus on becoming the best version of yourself, and the right people will naturally gravitate toward you. You deserve to surround yourself with those who lift you up, not those who weigh you down.

# CHAPTER 43
## The Law Of Accountability

Accountability is one of the most challenging lessons I've learned. At its core, it means taking responsibility for your actions, an idea that sounds simple yet is often anything but. Many people, regardless of gender, struggle with accountability because it demands an honest look in the mirror and an admission of faults, and that can feel uncomfortable. A lifetime of ingrained habits can make this self-reflection even harder.

Let me share a personal story. I had a drinking problem that turned me into someone I barely recognized. When I drank, I became spiteful and angry, revealing emotions I had buried for years. Only after I got sober did I face the truth: much of what happened in my life was my own doing. I blamed my ex-wife, past betrayals in the music industry, or any external circumstance I could find. It took a painful divorce to understand my role in the chaos. I had built a life around shortcuts, feeling entitled to happiness without putting in the effort.

The divorce was, in hindsight, one of the best things that ever happened to me. It forced me to confront my shortcomings and ask, "What did I do wrong?" That question captures the essence of accountability—facing problems head-on instead of avoiding them. You cannot go over them or under them; you have to go through them. Many people mask their struggles with substances or distractions, but that only delays the inevitable. Once the high fades or the diversion wears off, reality remains, often feeling more daunting than before.

I genuinely believe that everything that happens in your life is, in some way, your responsibility. Sure, uncontrollable events occur, like getting hit by a bus, but even then, a choice may have placed you in that situation. Accountability acts like a personal coach who refuses to let you off the hook. It lingers in your mind, urging you to examine each decision. If you are struggling financially, the problem is seldom just your job or bad luck; it often stems from your own choices. We are all dealt the same hand in life, yet some people thrive while others flounder, and the difference usually lies in the actions we take.

During my journey, I realized that until I accepted responsibility for my behavior, I could not change or grow. It takes courage to look in the mirror and ask, "What can I do better?" Accountability challenges you to face your dragons, whether they are financial struggles, health issues, or relationship problems. If you are overweight, commit to a gym routine. If you lack financial resources, seek new skills or education. If your relationships are suffering, reach out and build new connections.

The answers are already within us; we simply choose to ignore them. Complaining and gossiping might feel good in the moment, but those habits solve nothing. Jealousy and envy can be powerful emotions, yet they can be redirected into motivation. When someone else has what you desire, take it as proof of what you could achieve once you decide to act.

I remember being an overweight child, struggling with depression and low self-esteem. I had to confront the fact that my unhealthy lifestyle was holding me back. Embracing fitness became the turning point, gradually transforming my self-image. Likewise, I had to face my substance-abuse issues head-on. Once I quit drinking and drugs, my life changed dramatically. Within a year and a half, my financial situation improved, I restored relationships, and I gained the clarity that had eluded me for so long.

My experiences in accountability court taught me invaluable lessons about facing the consequences of my actions. I had to pay for my mistakes, both literally and figuratively. The process hurt, yet it instilled a sense of responsibility I had long neglected. I was forced to confront the anger, negativity, and destructive behavior that had harmed not only me but also the people around me.

The moral of this chapter is simple: unless you take ownership of your actions, growth remains elusive. Repeating the same mistakes because you avoid accountability leads only to frustration and stagnation. Life has a way of keeping the score, whether you notice it or not. The universe maintains a balance, and you will eventually experience the consequences of your choices, good or bad.

So, what are your dragons—financial, physical, emotional? The path to accountability may be difficult, but it is the only route to true transformation. Every step toward ownership opens doors to growth and change. Face your challenges, learn from them, and remember: accountability is the key to unlocking your potential.

# CHAPTER 44

## Seasons

Ah, the seasons of life—like a never-ending Netflix series, they keep rolling with plot twists that make you wonder if the writers have lost their minds. Just as the weather shifts outside, life comes with its own temperatures, moods, and awkward transitions. Picture it through a metaphor Mother Nature herself might applaud: the tree.

You plant a seed. In spring it sprouts, all green and hopeful. Summer arrives, and the young tree basks in the sun, soaking up rays like a beachgoer on a tropical holiday. When fall sweeps in, the tree throws a leaf-dropping party that feels a bit over the top. Winter follows, leaving it bare, standing there as if it just lost a bet. Yet the story is not over. The tree repeats this cycle season after season, just as life does.

Now let's get real. No one lives in an endless happy season; that is a myth, like unicorns or guilt-free pizza. Life tosses curveballs that could make a pro baseball player weep. You might enjoy a glorious summer, partying, meeting new people, and stacking some cash, but then, out of nowhere, you hit a rough patch. Relationships crumble, and you find yourself in a personal winter, staring at your phone as if it were the last slice of pizza, wondering where everyone went.

Take my personal journey, for example. I used to be married, and yes, I was someone's "better half," but now I'm enjoying life as a bachelor. I tell the women I date that I'm not looking for anything serious. During my brighter seasons I might juggle a few dates at once; think of me as a relationship magician. Inevitably, some realize we aren't in a fairy tale and disappear. Then come those barren winters when I'm alone with nothing but Netflix and a pint of ice cream. Yet that quiet stretch is my chance to grow.

Every season, even the hard ones, offers room for growth. Trees grow in silence, and so do we. Often no one notices your progress because you're working behind the scenes like a ninja in a dark room. Growth isn't usually loud; it's quiet and unseen. What are you doing when nobody's watching? Are you hitting the gym, learning a new skill, or building your side hustle? That's what separates winners from wannabes.

If you face your dark seasons with despair, they can feel like a never-ending winter that traps you in a snowstorm of negativity. Remember, the off-season is where real training happens. Just as in sports, what you do when the spotlight is off determines how you perform when it turns back on.

Think about the legends: Kobe Bryant, Michael Jordan, and Michael Jackson. They made success look effortless, yet we never sat in on their grueling off-season sessions. While the rest of us were binge-watching reality TV, they were alone in empty gyms and studios, practicing day in and day out.

Life moves in seasons, and it is vital to know which one you are in. Are you experiencing an off-season, a winning season, a learning season, or a growing season? Pinpointing your phase lets you adjust your mindset and actions accordingly. Remember, the journey is not a straight line to happiness; it is a roller-coaster ride of ups, downs, twists, and turns.

Hard times are just as valuable as the good ones because they teach us the sweet taste of victory. Without struggle, how could we ever appreciate success? Duality matters: light and dark, wins and losses. What truly defines you is how you navigate the setbacks, not just how you celebrate the triumphs.

When you feel alone in a pit of despair, remind yourself that this is only a test from the universe (God, cosmic forces, take your pick). It is a nudge to return to the work, stay humble, and keep evolving.

Consider the bamboo tree. For years it grows roots unseen beneath the soil before it ever shoots skyward; when it finally does, it rockets up. During those unseen years, it is just you and the mud; that is where real growth happens, below the surface, out of sight, just like your potential.

So, embrace each season. Whether you are enjoying a summer of abundance or enduring a winter of reflection, every phase has a purpose. Lean into the process, and remember that every tree needs a little mud to grow. Keep planting seeds, and let the seasons do their thing!

**Slay Your Demons**

Everyone has demons, those internal struggles that may seem trivial to others but loom large in our own lives. For me they were anger, drug addiction, and alcohol. To grow and become a productive member of society, I had to confront each one head-on. Ignoring them would have led me down a dark path, perhaps even to my demise. My demons are only one example; for others they might appear as procrastination, stagnation, fear of rejection, or even fear of success. The truth is simple: if you do not face your fears, they will haunt you indefinitely.

In my field of behavior analysis there is a technique called **systematic desensitization**, which involves gradually confronting your fears. I once worked with a client who was terrified of spiders. We started small by showing him pictures of spiders. At first he was distressed, but we slowly extended the time he spent looking at the images until he could manage a minute or two without panic. Next, we ventured outside, where he encountered a granddaddy long legs. His instinct was to run, yet over time he learned to tolerate their presence. Eventually we walked into the woods, where he faced even larger spiders. Despite my own discomfort I remained strong for him, and through this step-by-step process he completely conquered his fear.

This journey of slaying demons is similar to the age-old tale of confronting dragons. Each of us has dragons to face, and until we do we cannot claim victory in our lives. Demons can hold us tightly, not as supernatural beings from movies but as the nagging fears and anxieties that keep us from living fully. For example, I once longed to skydive. The idea terrified me, and I wanted to conquer that fear. Today I no longer feel the urge to jump out of a plane, but not because I am afraid; rather, I have come to value my life and the responsibilities that accompany it.

## Confronting Your Demons

Facing your demons is one of the most critical tasks you will undertake in life. If you allow them to fester, they will haunt you relentlessly, casting shadows over your potential and aspirations. Confronting and slaying these inner beasts is not merely an exercise in bravery; it is essential for personal growth and fulfillment. The process frees you from the chains of fear and enables you to build a life that aligns with your true desires. So, take the plunge: face your fears, confront your demons, and reclaim the life that is rightfully yours. The journey may be daunting, but the rewards of freedom and self-discovery justify every effort.

## Feelings and Logic

Welcome to the fascinating world of feelings and logic, a double-edged sword that can either elevate you or leave you in a heap of trouble. Let's face it: we all have feelings, and they are as natural as breathing. Here is the kicker, though: feelings can be as misleading as a cat pretending to love you moments before it knocks over your favorite plant. Emotions are energy in motion, yet they are fleeting and temporary. If you are not careful, they can steer you down some questionable paths.

Imagine this: your feelings might tempt you to stalk your ex on social media, convinced that a little digital sleuthing will rekindle an old flame. In a burst of emotion, you might even want to confront someone who "disrespected" you. Or perhaps you feel the all-too-tempting urge to skip work for a Netflix binge. Feelings can trigger chaotic decisions, but here is the twist: when you learn to analyze them, those same feelings can propel you toward personal growth.

First, take a clear-eyed look at what you are feeling. What hides behind that urge? Why do you feel this way? What events led you to this emotional state? This is where behavior analysis enters the picture. Think of it as detective work: identify the antecedent (what happened just before the feeling) and anticipate the consequences of any action you might take. One night of partying can lead to a lifetime of regret, or at the very least a hangover that feels like a freight train.

Feelings are powerful; they invite introspection and can nudge you in the right direction. They are energy that can be harnessed for manifestation, yet you need logic to channel that energy effectively. Picture your feelings as a loaded gun. You have likely heard the phrase "Guns don't kill people; people kill people." The same applies to feelings and logic: feelings provide the force, and logic decides where to aim.

Feelings flicker like a summer storm, arriving and departing in moments. Logic, by contrast, transcends time and helps you make choices that serve your future self. For instance, when you are out with friends and everyone is drinking, your feelings might shout, "Join the fun!" while your logic whispers, "Getting pulled over is a real possibility."

Here is the thing: feelings can hint at possible consequences, while logic helps you avoid them altogether. Imagine that an emotionally driven friend decides to drink and ends up with a DUI. Now compare that outcome with someone who relies on logic and chooses to stay sober. Which scenario sounds better? Spoiler alert: it is the one that avoids a court date and a hefty fine.

A balance between feelings and logic is essential. Without any emotional input, logic can become cold and calculating—picture those science-fiction stories in which robots conclude that humans pose a threat and decide to eliminate them. If those robots had feelings, they might see the beauty of mistakes and the value of learning from them.

Neither feelings nor logic is inherently superior; each plays a vital role. Feelings reveal what is needed, while logic examines those feelings and guides you toward informed decisions. Life rarely fits into neat categories of black and white. Instead, you search for the best answer among countless possibilities. If you let feelings alone drive your behavior, without any logical oversight, you can quickly spiral out of control.

So what is the takeaway? Feelings are indicators, not dictators. They provide insight into your emotional state, but logic grants the gift of self-control. You cannot manage everything around you, yet you can choose how to respond to your feelings.

Think of feelings and logic as partners in a dance, each essential to achieving harmony. Without the gun, there is no trigger to pull; without the person pulling the trigger, the gun remains inert. By learning to navigate the relationship between feelings and logic, you master the art of decision-making and lead a more balanced life. Embrace both your emotional and rational sides, and let them work together for your benefit.

**Perspective and Discernment**

Perspective and discernment are vital qualities that define a wise individual. To navigate life strategically, cultivating these traits is essential. Let us explore perspective first.

**Perspective** refers to the way you interpret and react to life's events. Challenges and unforeseen circumstances are inevitable, and your perception of them can greatly affect your emotional and mental well-being. Consider the experience of losing a significant other. You might spiral into despair, thinking, "I will never find someone else," or you could ask, "What can I learn from this? Perhaps the relationship was not meant for me, or maybe it is time to grow." The second viewpoint promotes healing and opens the door to new opportunities.

Your belief system carries immense power because what you think shapes your reality. This is not about being delusional; it is about choosing a mindset that serves you. Life is seldom a life-or-death situation, and the more weight you place on a negative event, the heavier it becomes. When faced with challenges such as losing a job, treat the moment as a chance for growth. Remind yourself that new opportunities will appear, and trust that the universe will provide. Dwelling in misery only prolongs suffering and leads to stagnation. By consciously focusing on the positive, you place yourself on a path toward recovery and future success.

## Discernment

Now, let's delve into **discernment**. While perspective centers on your internal dialogue, discernment means stepping into someone else's shoes. It's about understanding others' feelings and circumstances so you can make more empathetic decisions and build meaningful relationships. When people overlook another person's viewpoint, misunderstandings and conflict often follow.

Suppose someone cancels a date. It's easy to feel hurt or rejected, yet what if that person is dealing with a family emergency? A lack of discernment can spark unnecessary tension, while recognizing their situation fosters compassion and connection.

At its core, discernment is about respecting others. Despite the frustrations people sometimes cause, strive to honor their experiences and perspectives. A time-tested rule is to treat people as you'd like to be treated. This principle, commonly called the Golden Rule, reaches beyond individual relationships and extends to humanity as a whole. When we meet others with kindness and understanding, we help create a more compassionate world.

In the grand tapestry of life, we're all interconnected. Everyone carries personal burdens, and acknowledging this prevents us from becoming insensitive or dismissive. Something that seems trivial to you may hold great importance for someone else. Overlooking another person's struggle can erode relationships, while empathy and understanding allow connection to flourish.

When you develop both perspective and discernment, you create a powerful framework for handling your interactions. These qualities let you respond thoughtfully instead of reacting impulsively, deepening your understanding of the world around you. By honing them, you not only enrich your own life but also lift up the lives of others.

In essence, perspective and discernment are pillars of emotional intelligence. They help you rise above challenges, foster empathy, and build meaningful connections. Life isn't just about your experiences; it's also about understanding and respecting the experiences of those around you. Embrace these traits, and they'll light the way toward personal growth and fulfilling relationships.

**The Concept of Pain**

Ah, pain—the unwelcome guest who shows up uninvited at every party. Nobody likes it. It's the broccoli of life's buffet: you'd rather skip it, yet it turns out to be surprisingly good for you. Pain, in all its uncomfortable glory, is the best teacher you never asked for. Think of it as that blunt friend who tells you the truth when you'd rather hear sweet nothings.

Consider the miracle of childbirth. In that moment a mother's wracked with pain, yet from it new life appears. Pain is the catalyst for growth, and it's high time we learn to embrace it. In fact, pain's more valuable than pleasure. Why? Because it shows us what we need to change. Think of it as life's way of giving you a nudge (or a shove) in the right direction. Most people try to run away from pain, but by doing so they miss the lessons it offers.

Take a peek into the world of athletes. Ever seen someone bench-pressing like their life depends on it? That's pain at work. They endure discomfort in the gym to strengthen their muscles and gain an edge over the competition. Just like those athletes, we need to recognize that without a little pain, we can't grow. Pain's our honest friend, reminding us we may not be doing as well as we think.

If you don't choose your pain, life will choose it for you. Whether it's going back to school, writing the book you've been putting off, or simply saying "no" to unhealthy habits, the path of growth often feels unpleasant. Embrace it. Picture the caterpillar: it endures the pain of being small and vulnerable, dodging predators, then cocoons itself and emerges as a magnificent butterfly. Talk about a glow-up. This is the butterfly effect in action; without the struggle, you can't appreciate the beauty of transformation.

Let's get real: life's a roller-coaster, complete with highs and lows. If we only experienced joy, we wouldn't have a frame of reference for true happiness. Pain gives depth to our understanding of pleasure. Successful people often look back on their struggles and say, "I wouldn't change a thing," because those hardships shaped them into who they are today.

Loss is part of the human experience. Whether it's family, friends, jobs, or even your favorite pair of socks, losing something often brings a fresh perspective. Sacrifice naturally accompanies this process. In ancient times, people sacrificed animals (and sometimes each other, yikes!) in the name of growth. I'm not advocating bloodshed, but the principle remains: sometimes you've got to release old habits and relationships to make room for newer, healthier ones.

Pain can feel like a heavy burden, yet it's also a powerful catalyst for transformation. Sadly, some people can't handle it and take drastic measures because they don't see the bigger picture. God, or the universe if that's more your vibe, gives us these challenges to prepare us for greater things.

Here's a personal anecdote. I once received thirty thousand dollars with almost no effort on my part. I won't share the details (I don't want to get in trouble!), but without any struggle I had no idea how to value it. The money disappeared faster than a magician's rabbit because I treated it like an unlimited ticket to Fun Land. If I'd had to hustle and grind for it, I would've understood its worth. That's why many lottery winners end up broke: when you don't earn something, you don't learn how to keep it.

We usually see the good as inherently valuable, yet pain, fear, and loneliness are often the real treasures. When hardship hits, plenty of people cry, "Why me, God?" The answer's simple: He's trying to teach you something. God provides lessons, not just blessings. If we got everything we wanted, we'd wind up hopelessly lost.

So, let's make pain our friend! It's our greatest teacher, the professor we never asked for but desperately need. Pain guides us, shows us what we need to do, and reminds us that growth often comes through discomfort. Embrace it, learn from it, and you'll find pain isn't the enemy; it's the catalyst for your greatest transformation.

## The Concept of Fun

Ah, fun! The elusive, sparkly unicorn of adulthood that everyone seems to chase. There's even a catchy song, Girls Just Want to Have Fun, that insists girls just want it, but let's be real, who doesn't? Fun is usually equated with happiness, joy, and the sweet nectar of life. Before we dive headfirst into the pool of merriment, though, let's pause and ask whether fun is really as fabulous as it's cracked up to be. Spoiler alert: it might be a bit overrated.

As kids, fun is a magical realm where every day brings a new adventure. Remember those glorious games of tag until dusk or the trampoline sessions that sent you soaring like a superhero? The thrill of riding bikes, the excitement of going to the movies, and that blissful moment when you conquered the highest level of your favorite video game were priceless.

But as adults, our idea of fun often shifts to more *adulting* pursuits: drinking, smoking, questionable decisions, and that "wild night out" you're still regretting three days later.

Let's be honest: adult fun can feel like a double-edged sword. Sure, it's enjoyable, but it also comes with a hefty price tag. If I had a dollar for every time a night of "fun" turned into a morning of regret, I could probably fund my own amusement park. Fun can cost you money, time, and occasionally your freedom, because nothing says "good choice" like a night out that ends with a run-in with the law. Remember, kids: "fun" is not an acceptable defense in a court of law!

But here's the catch: fun isn't inherently bad; it's about balance. Fun should be a reward, not a constant state of being. Think of it like dessert: it's great to indulge occasionally, yet you wouldn't want cake for breakfast, lunch, and dinner. I've learned that true fun comes from accomplishments such as watching my daughter thrive, hitting goals I've set, or simply enjoying a well-deserved break after a long week. That's the kind of fun that won't leave you feeling like a bus ran over you the next day.

Now, let's not ignore that human nature craves pleasure. Our brains are wired to chase experiences that feel good, but sometimes we let our hearts lead us astray. Keep a tight leash on that wild heart of yours until your brain has a chance to weigh in. Remember, fun should be earned, not handed out like Halloween candy.

Picture a farmer who diligently plants his seeds, nurtures them, and waits for the harvest. When the time comes, he celebrates with a big slice of pie. That's how fun should work: put in the hard work and then savor the sweet reward.

While we're on the subject of social media, let's call out the elephant in the room. Those picture-perfect posts you scroll through are often just that, isolated moments. Don't let the snapshots fool you; behind every smiling face is a story you may not see. They could be having fun, sure, but they might also be fishing for likes. So don't fall into the FOMO trap. You're not missing out on anything. Stay on your path, keep working, and trust that fun will show up in its own time, just like that friend who always arrives uninvited.

I'm not saying you should shun fun altogether; I'm simply advocating a smart approach. Choose your fun wisely, and always weigh the possible consequences of your choices. Life is a delicate dance between hard work and enjoyment, and mastering that rhythm is what leads to real fulfillment. So go ahead, have fun, but keep one eye on the clock and the other on your goals. Here's to finding balance in the world of fun.

## Conclusion

As we reach the end of this journey together, remember the core message of this book: you're not alone, and you have the power to change your life. We all get stuck sometimes, trapped by the shadows of our past or paralyzed by the uncertainties of the future. Let this book be your guide to breaking that cycle and embracing the beauty of the present moment. After all, they call it the "present" for a reason; it's a gift waiting to be unwrapped.

Throughout these chapters, I've shared my own missteps and lessons learned, not from a pedestal of superiority, but as a fellow traveler on this winding road we call life. The truth is, the greatest among us often carry the heaviest baggage of mistakes. God, or whatever higher power you believe in, gives the toughest tests to those who are prepared to grow. If you've stumbled along the way, take heart; it means you're on the right track.

Life is a process, a series of trials and tribulations that shape us into who we're meant to be. It isn't about being the smartest or the most talented; it's about recognizing that everyone possesses unique gifts and skills that guide us along different paths. Completion doesn't come from perfection, but from embracing the journey itself.

The lessons in this book are meant to stand the test of time, offering universal truths that can guide you through life's ever-changing landscape. The most important takeaway is simple: you are enough. No matter how turbulent the world becomes, your worth remains constant, and you can make choices that enrich your life and the lives of those around you.

Life is never a perfectly smooth ride; it's filled with ups and downs, losses, and gains. You might lose relationships, possessions, or even your sense of self at times. Yet once you lose yourself, everything else becomes irrelevant. Time is the one resource you can't get back, so cherish it. This book exists to help you maximize that precious time and move toward a life of fulfillment.

I'm just an ordinary person with a deep appreciation for life's lessons, and I wrote this book for anyone who feels lost—the man who has wandered off course, the woman struggling to see her value, or anyone searching for meaning in a chaotic world. This isn't merely a motivational pep talk; it's a set of disciplines designed to enrich your experience.

Happiness isn't a constant state; it's something you cultivate through hard work and dedication. Although the title emphasizes "man," these insights are for everyone. My perspective as a man shapes the narrative, but the wisdom here transcends gender.

So, as you close this book, wake up each day with purpose. Set a goal, take action, and enjoy the ride. Life should be fun, but it's also about growth. Like a farmer tending seeds, you must nurture your dreams with time, effort, and love. Only then will you harvest the fruits of your labor.

In the end, giving matters as much as receiving. As you move forward, trust that the universe, or whatever you believe in, will reward your efforts. Step into the light, embrace the present, and let this moment mark the start of your transformation. You've got this!

# CHAPTER 45

## Protect Your Biggest Investment: You

In the grand tapestry of life, we often misplace the essence of real investment. We pour money into vacations, flashy lifestyles, or fleeting pleasures, convinced they'll deliver the biggest return. The truth is simpler: *you are your greatest investment*.

**Understanding Your Value**

Think of yourself as a rare diamond, unique and irreplaceable. Like a snowflake, no one else matches your exact pattern. That knowledge should spark a deep sense of worth. When you fail to protect this investment, you invite problems ranging from financial ruin to unhealthy relationships, or you let life drift away on a tide of poor choices.

**The Temptations We Face**

Reckless choices are easy to make, whether it's late nights in Las Vegas or substance abuse. We slip because we underestimate our own value. Each lingering regret chips at our confidence and steals from our future.

**Delayed Gratification**

Imagine directing resources toward self-improvement instead of quick thrills. Those who choose growth enjoy compound rewards. Saying no to distraction and yes to progress lets your investment flourish.

## Self-Parenting

Take charge of your life the way a caring parent guides a child. Admit past mistakes, learn from them, and steer clear of gambling or shallow relationships. Give your time, attention, and love to pursuits that develop your character.

## The Nature of Temptation

Think of temptation as the lower voice inside you, urging you toward fleeting pleasure. When you give in, you drift from your potential. Teachings found in sacred texts aren't mere fables; they're practical instructions on protecting both yourself and your most valuable asset.

## The Journey to Self-Realization

I've walked the path of self-destruction, throwing away money in strip clubs, drowning in alcohol, and neglecting my true self. It took time to see that I was my own worst enemy. Through self-discovery, I learned that I'm worthy of greatness, and achieving it means choosing actions that rise above the average.

## Time Is Your Asset

Time is a critical element of investment. When you squander it, you jeopardize your future. The way you handle small tasks reflects your overall mindset; if you let minutes slip away, every part of your life will mirror that loss.

## Investing in Yourself

Shift the narrative. Instead of pouring energy into others' demands, focus on your own growth. When you invest in yourself, you become a pillar of strength for everyone around you. This mindset is essential for escaping the cycle of modern-day slavery—working nonstop just to stay afloat.

**Mastery Over Self**

Life isn't merely about happiness or enjoyment; it's a quest for growth. Embrace self-mastery with a clear plan and steady dedication. Just as financial investments need cultivation, personal growth requires purposeful effort and consistent energy.

**Conclusion**

*You are the greatest asset you possess.* Protect and nurture that investment every day. Commit to self-improvement, and you'll create a more abundant life for yourself and for those you cherish. Invest wisely, and watch your life transform into something extraordinary.

By recognizing your worth and making deliberate choices, you can cultivate a life that flourishes and sets the stage for a legacy that inspires others. Are you ready to invest in the most valuable asset you have—yourself?

www.ingramcontent.com/pod-product-compliance
Lightning Source LLC
Chambersburg PA
CBHW041315120726
48005CB00014B/2010